First World War
and Army of Occupation
War Diary
France, Belgium and Germany

49 DIVISION
Divisional Troops
199 Machine Gun Company
13 December 1916 - 31 October 1917

WO95/2787/2

The Naval & Military Press Ltd
www.nmarchive.com
Published in association with The National Archives

Published by

The Naval & Military Press Ltd

Unit 10 Ridgewood Industrial Park,

Uckfield, East Sussex,

TN22 5QE England

Tel: +44 (0) 1825 749494

www.naval-military-press.com

www.nmarchive.com

This diary has been reprinted in facsimile from the original. Any imperfections are inevitably reproduced and the quality may fall short of modern type and cartographic standards.

© **Crown Copyright**
Images reproduced by permission of The National Archives, London, England, 2015.

Contents

Document type	Place/Title	Date From	Date To
Heading	WO95/2787/3 199 Machine Gun Company		
Heading	49th Division 199th Machine Gun Coy. Dec 1916-Oct 1917 From U.K To Italy Nov 17 41 Division.		
Heading	War Diary Of 199th Machine Gun Company. For December 1916 Vol I		
War Diary	Grantham	13/12/1916	13/12/1916
War Diary	En Route	14/12/1916	15/12/1916
War Diary	Le Havre	16/12/1916	17/12/1916
War Diary	En Route	18/12/1916	18/12/1916
War Diary	Grouches	19/12/1916	30/12/1916
Heading	War Diary Of 199 Machine Gun Company For January 1917 Vol 2		
Heading	War Diary Of For 1917		
War Diary	Grouches	30/12/1916	08/01/1917
War Diary	Humbercamps	09/01/1917	29/01/1917
Miscellaneous	No. 199. Machine Gun Company. Operation Orders. No I for 8-1-17 By Captain J Muhlig M.C. Commanding 199 M.G. Coy	07/01/1917	07/01/1917
Heading	War Diary Of 199th Machine Gun Company For February 1917 Vol 3		
War Diary	Humbercamps	30/01/1917	26/02/1917
Miscellaneous	No. 199 Machine Gun Company Operation Orders No 2 By Captain J. Muhlig M.C. Commanding 199 M.G. Coy	25/02/1917	25/02/1917
Miscellaneous	No 199 Machine Gun Company Operation Orders No 3 By Captain J. Muhlig M.C. Commanding 199 M.G. Coy	28/02/1917	28/02/1917
Heading	War Diary. Of 199th Machine Gun Company For March 1917 Vol 4		
War Diary	Bouquemaison	24/02/1917	28/02/1917
War Diary	Bouquemaison En Route Hernicourt	01/03/1917	01/03/1917
War Diary	Hernicourt En Route Aumerval	02/03/1917	02/03/1917
War Diary	Aumerval in Route Haverskirque	03/03/1917	03/03/1917
War Diary	Haverskirque En Route La Grand Pacaut.	04/03/1917	04/03/1917
War Diary	Le Grand Pacaut En Route Laventie	05/03/1917	05/03/1917
War Diary	Laventie	06/03/1917	30/03/1917
Operation(al) Order(s)	No 199 Machine Gun Company. Operation Orders. No. 4. By Captain J. Muhlig Commanding 199 M.G. Coy.	02/03/1917	02/03/1917
Operation(al) Order(s)	No 199 Machine Gun Company. Operation Orders. No. 5. By Captain J. Muhlig Commanding 199 M.G. Coy.	02/03/1917	02/03/1917
Operation(al) Order(s)	No 199 Machine Gun Company. Operation Orders. No. 6. By Captain J. Muhlig M.C. Commanding 199 M.G. Coy.	04/03/1917	04/03/1917
Miscellaneous	No 199 (Div) Machine Gun Company. Operation Orders. No. 7. By Captain J. Muhlig M.C. Commanding 199 M.G. Coy.	10/03/1917	10/03/1917
Miscellaneous	No 199 Machine Gun Company. Operation Orders. No. 8. By Capt J. Muhlig M.C. Commanding 199 M.G. Coy.	16/03/1917	16/03/1917

Miscellaneous	No 199 Machine Gun Company. Operation Orders. No. 9. By Capt J. Muhlig M.C. Commanding 199 M.G. Coy.	22/03/1917	22/03/1917
Heading	War Diary. Of 199th Machine Gun Coy For April 1917 Vol 5		
War Diary	Laventie	31/03/1917	05/04/1917
War Diary	Le Touret	06/04/1917	11/04/1917
War Diary	Trenches Fine du Bois Sect	12/04/1917	20/04/1917
War Diary	Les Huits Maison	21/04/1917	27/04/1917
War Diary	Trenches Neuve Chapelle Sector	28/04/1917	29/04/1917
Miscellaneous	No. 199 Machine Gun Company Operation Orders. No. 11 By Captain J. Muhlig M.C. Commanding 199 M.G. Coy	04/04/1917	04/04/1917
Miscellaneous	199 Machine Gun Company.	04/04/1917	04/04/1917
Miscellaneous	From Officer Commndg 199 Machine Gun Coy To Hdqs 49th Division A Branch	31/05/1917	31/05/1917
War Diary	Trenches Neuve Chapelle Sector	30/04/1917	13/05/1917
War Diary	Reserve Billets Viele Chapelle	14/05/1917	15/05/1917
War Diary	Reserve Billets Zelobes	16/05/1917	21/05/1917
War Diary	Trenches Fauquissart Sector	22/05/1917	30/05/1917
War Diary	In the field	31/05/1917	31/05/1917
Heading	War Diary. Of 199th Machine Gun Coy For June 1917 Vol 7		
War Diary	Trenches Fauquissart Sector	31/05/1917	04/06/1917
War Diary	Divisional Reserve Billets Zelobes	05/06/1917	14/06/1917
War Diary	Reserve Billets Zelobes	15/06/1917	15/06/1917
War Diary	Divisional Reserve Billets Zelobes	16/06/1917	16/06/1917
War Diary	Trenches Fme du Bois Sector	17/06/1917	29/06/1917
Heading	War Diary 199. M G Coy July 1917 Vol 8		
War Diary	Trenches Fme du Bois Sector	30/06/1917	10/07/1917
War Diary	Billets Le Touret	11/07/1917	11/07/1917
War Diary	Vendin Lez Bethune	12/07/1917	13/07/1917
War Diary	Leffrinckhoucke Nr Dunkerque	14/07/1917	16/07/1917
War Diary	Oost Dunkerque	17/07/1917	17/07/1917
War Diary	Nieuport	18/07/1917	30/07/1917
Heading	199 M.G. Coy. War Diary August 1917 Vol 9		
War Diary		31/07/1917	30/08/1917
Miscellaneous	199 Machine Gun Coy	08/08/1917	08/08/1917
Heading	War Diary of 199 Machine Gun Coy for September 1917		
War Diary		31/08/1917	10/09/1917
War Diary	Bray Dunes	11/09/1917	30/09/1917
Miscellaneous	From O.C 199 M Coy To Headquarters 41th Divisional (g)	31/10/1917	31/10/1917
War Diary		01/10/1917	31/10/1917
Miscellaneous	Report of operations carried out by the 199th Machine Gun Company during period 5th-11th October 1917	05/10/1917	05/10/1917

WO/95/3287/3

199 Machine Gun Company.

49TH DIVISION

199TH MACHINE GUN COY.
DEC 1916-OCT 1917

FROM UK

TO ITALY NOV 17
41 DIVISION

49TH DIVISION

Vol I.

SECRET.

WAR DIARY.

OF

199th Machine Gun Company.

FOR

December. 1916.

Army Form C. 2118.

WAR DIARY of No. 199. Machine Gun Company

DECEMBER 1916.

INTELLIGENCE SUMMARY

(Erase heading not required.)

Instructions regarding War Diaries and Intelligence Summaries are contained in F. S. Regs., Part II. and the Staff Manual respectively. Title Pages will be prepared in manuscript.

Place	Date	Hour	Summary of Events and Information	Remarks and references to Appendices
GRANTHAM	12/12/16		The Company entrained for Service Overseas, leaving BELTON PARK at 11.50 p.m. Strength of Company 10 offrs 144 other Ranks.	
EN ROUTE	14/12/16		Arrived at SOUTHAMPTON at 12.50 p.m. Embarked on S.S. HUNTSCRAFT at 8 p.m.	
EN ROUTE	15/12/16		A quiet voyage, arrived at LE HAVRE about 9 a.m., dis-embarked about 2 p.m. & received orders to proceed to No. 1. Rest Camp. Receive R.S. Wagon & 1.A.S.C. driver, 2 heavy draught horses. Strength of Coy 10 offrs 148 other Ranks.	
LE HAVRE	16/12/16		The day was spent in Rest Camp, completing equipment & cleaning up. Weather bad, rain & cold.	
LE HAVRE	17/12/16		The Company received orders to entrain for the front, entraining at POINT 3. at 6 p.m., destination DOULLENS.	
EN ROUTE	18/12/16		Day spent in Train, arrived DOULLENS at 9.30 p.m., de-trained & marched to next billets at GROUCHES. Settled in Billets about 11 p.m. Casualties Nil.	
GROUCHES	19/12/16		The Company became part of the 1 & 9th (West Riding) Divisions Day was spent cleaning up & inspection billets, parschal, etc. Casualties Nil. Strength of Company 10 offrs 148 other Ranks	P.T.O

Army Form C. 2118.

WAR DIARY of N° 199 Machine Gun Coy.
INTELLIGENCE SUMMARY

(Erase heading not required.)

December 1916.

Instructions regarding War Diaries and Intelligence Summaries are contained in F.S. Regs., Part II. and the Staff Manual respectively. Title Pages will be prepared in manuscript.

Place	Date	Hour	Summary of Events and Information	Remarks and references to Appendices
Grouches	20/12/16		Nominal Roll of Officers :-	
			Capt. MUHRIG, J. Commanding.	
			Lieut. HARVEY R.J. 2/in Command.	
			— PORTER C.V. Sec⁰ off. No. 1.	
			— ASQUITH G. ,, ,, ,, 2.	
			2/Lieut ADAM D.B. ,, ,, ,, 3.	
			— LINDLEY A.C. ,, ,, ,, 4.	
			— FISHER E.J. Sub Sec⁰ off. N°1.	
			— BARKER W.P. ,, ,, ,, 2.	
			— THORPE W.F. ,, ,, 3rd Trans off.	
			— ELSON R. ,, ,, ,, 4.	
			The day was occupied Training. A fine cold day.	
			Casualties 1. Other Ranks to F.Amb.	
			Strength of Coy: 10 Offrs: 148 O.R.	
Grouches	21/12/16		Weather dull, rain during day. Training Resumed. No events of importance	
			Strength of Coy: 10 Offrs 148 Other Ranks. Inspection of Ammo by Col Verge.	
Grouches	22/12/16		A wet day. Training resumed outdoors in intervals of dry weather.	
			No events of Importance. Strength of Coy: 10 Offrs: 148 Other Ranks (1 Field Ambulance)	
Grouches	23/12/16		A wet day. Training resumed. C. O's Kit + Equip inspection. A quiet day.	R.T.O
			Strength of Coy: 10 Offrs: 148 Other Ranks (1 Field Ambulance O.R.)	

Army Form C. 2118.

WAR DIARY of No 199 Machine Gun Company
DECEMBER 1916 or INTELLIGENCE SUMMARY

(Erase heading not required.)

(3)

Instructions regarding War Diaries and Intelligence Summaries are contained in F. S. Regs., Part II. and the Staff Manual respectively. Title Pages will be prepared in manuscript.

Place	Date	Hour	Summary of Events and Information	Remarks and references to Appendices
GROUCHES	24/12/16		Wet & cold, Divine service, Company to Baths, Moved Transport Lines. Strength of Company 10 Officers 148 O.R. (1 field ambulance)	
GROUCHES	25/12/16		Wet & Mild, lecture services, A quiet day.	
GROUCHES	26/12/16		Fine morning, rain during evening, Route March during morning, no evacuation. Tactical exercise during afternoon. Sick normal. Strength of Coy 10 officers 148 O.Rs (1 Field Ambulance.)	
Groudres	27/12/16		Fine dry training resumed in Training Area. (Tactical Exercises) Sick Enturned, all minor ailments. Offr Adam sick in Billets Strength of Coy 10 offrs 148 O. Ranks. (1 Bear Rest Station)	
Granches	28/12/16		A fine cold day, training resumed, company seen at work by Army Commdt Sick Nil. Strength of Company 10 offrs 148 O Rs. (1 ort Rear Station.	
Granches	29/12/16		A wet forenoon, Training resumed in Billets. Sick One, Strength of Company 10 offrs 148 O.Rs (1 Our Rest Stn)	
GROUCHES 30-12-16				

Anell Capt
Commdg 199 M.G. Coy.

Vol 2

SECRET.

WAR DIARY.

OF

199 Machine Gun Company

FOR

January.

1917.

SECRET.

WAR DIARY

OF

FOR

1917.

Army Form C. 2118.

Page 1.

WAR DIARY
of No 199. MACHINE GUN COMPANY.
INTELLIGENCE SUMMARY
(Erase heading not required.)

For JANUARY 1917.

Place	Date	Hour	Summary of Events and Information	Remarks and references to Appendices
GROUCHES	30/12/16		A fine day. Inspection of Equipment & Kit held in Billets during forenoon, afternoon spent improving Billets & Mule Lines. 2/Lieut WARNER rejoined company from RW Rest Station, quite better. Health of company good. Str Nil. Strength of Coy. 10 offrs 148 O.Rs.	McK
GROUCHES	31/12/16		A fine day, cold. Company attended Divine Service during morning, taken by Div Chaplain. Afternoon company rested. Scr Nil. Strength of Company 10 offrs 148 O.Rs.	Incokt.
GROUCHES	1/1/17		Roll of Officers on 1st Capt. J. MUHLIE. Comm'dg Coy. Medr. R.J. HARLEY. 2nd in Command — C.W. PORTER. Comm'dg "A" Sect. — G. ASQUITH. — "B" — 2.Lieut D.B. ADAM. — "C" — — A.C. LINDLEY. — "D" — — E.J. FISHER. Sub Section Comm'dr "A" Section — W.P. BARKER. — "B" — — N.F. THORPE. — "C" — & Transport Offr — R. ELSON. — "D" — New year commenced with slight rain, but cleared up during afternoon. Very mild. The Coy was inspected by the CORPS M.G.O (Lt Col HENDERSON) & first seen drawn up in inspection order. He was satisfied with physique & general bearing of the men, Sections afterwards endeavoured to work, each Section carrying out work according to his orders. Report very satisfactory. Company departed at 11.15 am. After inspecting Billets, office shops, mule lines etc. having remarked of day Training was resumed in Billets. Improved with the importance of having at least 1 hr per diem at "Immediate Action" a most necessary part of training. Str Nil. Strength of Company 10 offrs 148 Other Ranks.	Muht
GROUCHES	2/1/17		Weather fair inclined to Rain. 40 men with proportion of N.C.Os working party, Sanitation of Village. Remainder of Coy. spent day on Training Area. Section schemes easily Sub No Sections also. Beef & bowl extra, did them a lot of good. O.C. Coy attended a demonstration with FARQUHAR-HILL Rifle. Str Nil. Strength of Company 10 offrs 148 O.Rs.	Muht

Army Form C. 2118.

WAR DIARY
or
INTELLIGENCE SUMMARY

(Erase heading not required.)

Page. 5. N°. 199. MACHINE GUN CORPS.

for JANUARY 1919

Place	Date	Hour	Summary of Events and Information	Remarks and references to Appendices
2 ROUCHES	3/1/19		Weather fair, slight showers of rain throughout day. On the day men proceeded to BATHS at LUCHEUX, change of clothing. Interval of bathing spent training in BULLETS, combined drill which I think is very necessary to keep men active in handling the gun & keeping the mind alert. Sick 1. (Sgt MURPHY) to Field Ambulance. Received news of escape of 6 P.o.W. Company. Strength of Company 10 Offrs 148 O.Rs. (1 Field Ambulance).	(Illegible)
2 ROUCHES	4/1/19		Weather fair, rain during forenoon, afternoon fine. Training resumed on training area. Company exercise carried out. Results good, some men a little backward in pressing on trigger. Good information noticed in MULE LINES, all standing shipshape, a great advantage. Sick Nil. Strength of Coy 10 Offrs 148 O.Rs. C (1 Field Ambulance until files).	(Illegible)
2 ROUCHES	5/1/19		Weather cold & dry. Held & tested Box Respirators under N.C.O. from Div. Gas School. While company passed through Gas Chamber. (which a mighty). Respirators all tested. Company medically inspected by M.O. of Artillery Bde. found free from infectious diseases. Received Instrn (Operation orders) N° 93. (Re-move into line). Sick Nil. Strength of Company 10 Offrs 148 Other Ranks (1 Field Amb.) A very uneventful day.	(Illegible)
2 ROUCHES	6/1/19		Weather cold & fine, slight rain towards evening. Weekly kit harness & equipt inspection held. The overseas took second leave. Leaving ENGLAND have fell to precisely or army tally. Daily working party out today to 20 men. Communion service held by Div. Chaplain. A Sick Nil, Lucelles Nil. Strength of Company 10 Offrs 148 O.Rs. (1 Field Ambulance.)	(Illegible)
2 ROUCHES	7/1/19		Weather fine & mild. Divine Service today by Div. Chaplain. A mule strayed during night, caught during forenoon after wandering near DOULLENS. Operation Order N° I issued, (copy to diary). Sgt MURPHY transferred to Brit Rest Stn. Strength of Coy 10 Offrs 148 O.Rs. (1 DRS)	(Illegible)

WAR DIARY

Army Form C. 2118.

Page No. 10.

INTELLIGENCE SUMMARY of No 199. MACHINE GUN COMPANY.

for JANUARY 1914

Place	Date	Hour	Summary of Events and Information	Remarks and references to Appendices
GROUCHES	8/1/14		Weather, Cold & Wet. Gloomy. Rain when however held off until arrival of company at destination. According to operation orders the Company paraded & left GROUCHES. by Route March for HUMBERCAMPS. Marched via (POMMERA – SAUDIEMPRE. Saulwing at HUMBERCAMPS at 3 p.m. No casualties on route, men marched well, no trouble with animals or limbers. Time taken 3½ hours. Billeting Party under 2/Lt HARLEY went on ahead. The company was allotted billets in B CAMP. 2 end of village. Officers Billets in village. Dug Hd Qrs at Billet No 63. Men very unsettled during night, no conditions for them. Animals under cover in cart in centre of village. Limbers near Camp. A quiet night. Sick Nil. Casualties Nil. Strength of Company 10 officers 148 other Ranks. (1 Pvl Reat Sn).	[signature]
HUMBERCAMPS	9/1/14.		Weather, Cold & Dry. By daylight AEIE of Camp revealed very filthy, full of ancient rubbish, no latrines. Day was spent cleaning up camp & making latrines, built cook-house, reading room, repairs finished. E.S. Wagon & horses sent to CROVE to Divisional Train. Sgt MURPHY from D.R.S. to Coy & S/Sgt Smith. Struck off strength. Sgt WILLIAMS to Transport. L/Sgt HOGBIN to A/Sgt. A quiet day, & night in the village. Sick Nil. Strength of Company 10 offs 148 Other Ranks.	[signature]
HUMBERCAMPS	10/1/14.		Weather cold, clear during afternoon. Forenoon spent in cleaning up, sanitation, repairing of camp. Divisional operation orders No 94 issued. In connection with these O.C. Coy proceeded to Brig Hd Qrs @ 11 a.m. 11 & 11.18 am respectively with G.S.O.1. & Capt M.S.O. M.G. Cop Programme arranged. 199 Coy evacuated from spartan. At 12 noon the company received its baptism of fire, hostile guns putting a salvo of 8 shells (calibre?) into the CAMP. Casualty 2 Casualties. Men quiet Steady & undisturbed. The afternoon was quiet generally. At 4.10 pm CAMP was again shelled a salvo of 10 Rds. (4.1 calibre.) 1 man slightly wounded, 1 man carried through falling into trench cover, otherwise a quiet night. Sick Nil. Casualties 3 other Ranks wounded. (Cpl FORD. Pte GOURLAY, Pte HALL 32 (Pte HALL 32 Evacuated to Dressing Station). Strength of Company 10 offs 145 Other Ranks.	[signature]
HUMBERCAMPS	11/1/14.		Weather cold, showers of sleet at intervals. During forenoon, Company proceeded on Route March, also Lewis Gun team during afternoon practiced with FRENCH OVERBALLE M/G. very strenuous & heavy, practical work of instructed meantime. Quite a useful article, men arrive on 24 hrs leave. O.C. Coy reconnoitred Regd Sector of Divisional line in company with O.E. 11.7. M.G. Coy Pte RILEY to Field Ambulance (injured to 10th inst badly hurt.) Casualties Nil. Strength of Company 10 offs 145 Other Ranks (1 Field Amb).	[signature]

Army Form C. 2118.

WAR DIARY

INTELLIGENCE SUMMARY of No 199. MACHINE GUN COMPANY.

for JANUARY. 1914.

Page No. 4.

Place	Date	Hour	Summary of Events and Information	Remarks and references to Appendices
HUMBERCAMP.	12/1/14		Weather Mild, Slight falls of Snow during day. During forenoon Gun drill was carried out, afternoon Retaliatory Divisional Artillery, assisted by M.G. Coys Nos. 144 & 148 carried out demonstration against hostile wire & trenches. 3 Offrs & 3 Sgts of company proceeded to Brig. Coys to assist & observe demonstration, remainder busy in training. Brig. Commander proceeded to HD Qrs 144 Bg M G Coy at Pommier, re defence of NoMansLand & for Rifle Section. 3 A quiet day in Camp, no shelling. Sick No. Casualties Nil. Strength of Coy 10 Offrs 145 O.Rs (IFA)	Appendx
HUMBERCAMP	13/1/14		A cold day. Snow fell during day. Improvement carried out in Camp. During forenoon, during afternoon sections held Gas Drill & Lecture. Underhand fully their Box Respirators nob. O.C. Coy in company with O.C. 146 Brig M G Coy reconnoitred Trench Sector of divisional front. A quiet day in Billets. also a quiet night. Sick Nil. Casualties Nil. Strength of Company 10 Offrs 145 Other Ranks (1 Field amb)	Appendx
HUMBERCAMP	14/1/14		Weather Cold & wet. Sections carried out Route March during forenoon, during afternoon carried out infantry drill & Revolver practise. Both theatre forms of training are very essential as it is very noticable how soon the appearance of the new Reinforcements to Ad Qrs 148 Brig at BASSEUX from their recommended abl's & left facilities for drill M G & fire. O.C Coy with 2/Lt FISHER. proceeded to BRIGADIER 4 Coy Commdr Annual good facilities for drill M G & fire sector of Div limits in company with B.Whik. Sick Nil. Strength & Company 13 Offrs 145 Other Ranks (1 Field Ambulance) A quiet day. & night in Billets.	Appendx
HUMBERCAMP	15/1/14		Weather Cold & Wet. Sections carried out Section Scheme (Open warfare) during forenoon, during Afternoon feet greasing & Lecture on Sanitation & Hygiene. Laming afternoon men bathed by sections. O.C. to division (during) forenoon to report results of reconnaissances. Sick 2 (Slight Ailments) Animals inspected by Vet Offr. Strength of Company 10 Offrs 145 Other Rks (IFA)	Appendx
HUMBERCAMP	16/1/14		Weather Cold & Wet. Sections tractors overhead & indirect fire during forenoon. Route March - afternoon. Company quite familiar with surrounding country. A quiet day & night in Billets. O.C. Day to Brig Hd Qrs to arrange relief of 144 Coy by 199. Coy. at 3.30 pm received news of cancellation of Relief. Coy required for other duties. Snow fell during night. 2/Lt FISHER promoted Temp Lieut. Sick Nil Strength of Company. 10 Offrs 145. Other Ranks (1 Field Amb).	Appendx

WAR DIARY or INTELLIGENCE SUMMARY

Army Form C. 2118.

of No. 199. MACHINE GUN COMPANY.

for JANUARY 1917.

Place	Date	Hour	Summary of Events and Information	Remarks and references to Appendices
HUMBERCAMP	14/1/17		Weather Mild. Snowing all day. Gun work carried on in Huts. Lectures on General Routine, Trenches etc. during afternoon. Company was inspected by M.O. 4 W.R. Regt. Found free from scabies. A quiet day, & night in Billets, no hostile shelling near village. Our guns busy during night. Received instructions from Divison as to work the company is intended to do and arrange work. Sick Nil. Strength of Company 10 Offrs 145 other Ranks. (1 Field Ambulance)	Present
HUMBERCAMP	18/1/17		A cold day, snow at intervals. Company practised Rest of Trench & Overhead Mounting during day. All ammo. fogged this day. Visit from Capt. E.S. and Lt HARTLEY to their M.G.E 41-11-16 & during evening, LECROFT taken bad with spasms in throat, to doctor. A quiet day & night in billets. Strength of Coy 10 Offrs 145 Other Ranks (1 D.R.S.) Sick 1. Pt RILEY from F.A. to b.R.S.	Present
HUMBERCAMP	19/1/17		A fine day, very cold, turf dry. Sections carried out Route March during forenoon. Practised Tactics afternoon. Geo alert on. Quiet day & night in Billet area. Pt RILEY rejoined Coy from our Rest Stn. LECROFT to Field Ambulance. Strength of Company 10 Offrs 145 Other Ranks (1 Field amb).	Present
HUMBERCAMP	20/1/17		Weather cold & fine, frost during night. Geo Alert on. Company spent forenoon & section Route March. O.C. Coy proceeded to Hd Qrs 147 M.G. Coy, BERLES to arrange details for attaching of men & eqpt for instructional. Hostile artillery active throughout day, shelling village & vicinity of HUMBERCAMP heavy. Shells intermittently during the day. Mostly shells from 105 mm. guns. No casualties amongst company but Inf. Battn in village suffered. Night quiet except for activity of our own guns. Strength of Company 10 Offrs 145 Other Ranks (1 Field Ambulance) Sick 1.	Present
HUMBERCAMP	21/1/17		A cold day, freezing but dry. Company carried out section Schemes during forenoon afternoon spent in bomb throwing etc. Lieuts PORTER, FISHER, + 12 other Ranks proceeded to W. Anti Aircraft Battery at LATTRE ST QUENTIN for 10 days course of instruction on Anti aircraft duties. Marched off at 10 p.m. O.C. Company proceeded to Hd Qrs of the 2 M.G. Corps at BAVIELLMONT + GROSVILLE respectively to arrange details Sick 1. & Pt Hunt to Field Ambulance. A quiet day in HUMBERCAMP also a quiet night. Strength of Company 10 Offrs 145 Other Ranks (2 Field Ambulance)	Present

WAR DIARY

INTELLIGENCE SUMMARY of No. 199. MACHINE GUN COMPANY

for JANUARY. 1917.

Army Form C. 2118.

Page No. 9.

Place	Date	Hour	Summary of Events and Information	Remarks and references to Appendices
HUMBERCAMPS	22/1/17		Weather, Cold & Finer. At 9 a.m. 2/Lt BARKER & 20 other ORs of No 2 Section, 2/Lieut ELSON & 20 other ORs No 4 Section. Proceeded into line for instruction of experience in Trenches being attached to 1st/6th, 1/7th, & 1/8 M.G. Coys respectively. Men very eager to get into trenches. All arrangements re. Rationing etc. made. SGT. N.E.O. & men for duties of gun upkeep Parties reached destinations safely, & settled down in line. On Return 2/Lt H.Y.R. attached as Shoemaker. Sgt. Kd. Casualties Nil. A quiet day in village & vicinity. Both artillery active throughout day, especially in the evening. Strength of Company 10 Off. = 146 other Ors. (2 field ambulances).	(signature)
HUMBERCAMPS	23/1/17		Weather Very Cold. Snow during afternoon. Aeroplane activity during morning. 2/Lt HARTLEY, 2/Lt ASQUITH, C.S.M. got to No.RFS & 12 O.R. around line held by 1/4 Coy. Received information that Division we transferred to VIII Corps. got to Village intermittently shelled throughout day, about 12 shells 105 m.m., no damage done. Reports from Trenches report that men in Trenches doing well, Received news from M/PARKER, writes doing well. Representative of 1/4 & 1/8 Coys. & here to. Artillery activity throughout day & night, but Billets quiet during night. 10 Off = 146 other ORs. (2 field Ambulances) Casualties Nil. Sir GW. Strength of Company.	(signature)
HUMBERCAMPS	24/1/17		Weather very cold but fine. Frost continues. Aeroplane activity throughout day. Artillery activity throughout day. 2/Lt HARTLEY & LINDLEY & M.D. Oss. 1/4 & Coy. at GROSVILLE returned from 1/4 Coy. 2/Lt HARTLEY & LINDLEY to look round & get things settled. Right men in Trenches doing well. Quiet in village & vicinity. Artillery letters throughout night. Sick Nil. Casualties Nil. Strength of Company 10 Off = 146 the other Ranks. (2 field Ambulances)	(signature)
HUMBERCAMPS	25/1/17		Weather very cold. Frost continues. Aeroplane activity throughout forenoon. Spare men of Company Revs. March during afternoon. 2/Lt HARTLEY, 2/Lt LENTH, 2/Lt ASQUITH & 2/Lt LINDLEY & R/Qtl. & LINDLEY to left, Leceive of time to get information of men in trenches & in line. Second from Men in trenches doing well. Quiet settled down, Think it will do them a great deal of good being in line. Second from L/PARKER, Clav. doing well. Next of Kin Roll checked & brought up to date. Our artillery fairly active throughout day. Machine clipped our during day Machine clipped mules during night. A quiet day in village & vicinity. No hostile shelling. 2 Mules clipped our during day. Machine clipped mules during night. Sick Nil, Le Croft & Stanford, to Rol Reat Station. Casualties Nil. Strength of Company 10 Off/146 ORs (it in 1 RPS)	(signature)
HUMBERCAMPS	26/1/17		Weather very cold. Frost continues. Snow during afternoon. Company Revolver Practice during morning. "B" Coy & "D" WARD 84 Casualties clearing Station 2/Lt Coy to issue Rev. as above in matter, kindly & Thorpe to the R.A.F. to our day sorts. Scot. Le Croft from D.R.S. to duty. Our Artillery active throughout forenoon but artillery active throughout day, enemy recently to first Re-enforcements (1 Runner) Posts to our 1st Section. Sgt. Bumilly Rd. Strength of Company 10 Off. 146 other Ranks (1 field ambulance)	(signature)
HUMBERCAMPS	27/1/17		Weather Cold & Draught. Frost continues. Further Cold E Wind during day. Company Revolver Practice & drill billet area.	

Army Form C. 2118.

WAR DIARY
or
INTELLIGENCE SUMMARY of N° 199. MACHINE GUN COMPANY.

(Erase heading not required.)

PAGE 10

Instructions regarding War Diaries and Intelligence Summaries are contained in F.S. Regs., Part II. and the Staff Manual respectively. Title Pages will be prepared in manuscript.

1st JANUARY. 1914.

Place	Date	Hour	Summary of Events and Information	Remarks and references to Appendices
HUMBERCAMPS	28/1/17		Our Artillery & hostile artillery active throughout day. Lt ADAM returned to Coy from 111th Coy. Sick to lay up. O.C. Coy to 8th Div. HQ Coy. Lt LINDSEY to 111th Coy in G.M section for a Reconnaissance. Pk PARK to Field Ambulance (S.I.P) Company to Baths during afternoon. Revolver practice during afternoon. Lt ADAMs rejoined from 3rd Army School of Cookery. A quiet day on village & Bullets, no hostile shelling. Rations did not arrive from Re-filling point until 8 p.m. Selected & attached Officers & Men for 2nd Course Anti-aircraft work. SICK: 1. Casualties Nil. Strength of Coy 10 Offrs 146 other Ranks (2 Sick out)	[initials]
HUMBERCAMPS	29/1/17		Weather Cold, frost continues. Atmosphere bright. Artillery activity during day. Lt HARLEY to BAVINCOURT for Cash. Company Re-Section during afternoon. Afternoon spent overhauling guns & ammunition. Very necessary living in/out weather. Fairly out during evening. A quiet day in other village & Bullets. SICK Nil. Casualties Nil. Strength of Coy 10 Offrs 146 other Ranks (2 Sick out)	[initials]
HUMBERCAMPS	30/1/17		Weather Cold, frost continues. Removal of accumulation of old Manure from Mule lines commenced. Lt/110 RPS to RP 10 Mules & 2 Horses to Mangle Bath Company. Route March during afternoon, Revolver Practice & bath during afternoon. Lt ASQUITH, ADAMS to BERLE, LT HARLEY for Reconnaissance of limits Dormann ~ W/Sharps. Quiet during a fairly quiet night. SICK Nil. Casualties Nil Strength of Company 10 Offrs 146 other Ranks (2 Sick Out)	[initials]

[signatures]
Commanding 199 MG Company

In the field
30-1-17

Copy No. 1.   Coy Form 1

NO. 199. MACHINE GUN COMPANY.

OPERATION ORDERS.   No. 1 for 8/1/19 By
Captain J. MUHLIG. M.C. Commanding 199 M.G. Coy.

At GROUCHES.   Dated 4-1-19.

1.	REFERENCE MAPS Sheet 510 & 54b 1/40000 Ref D.H. Operation Orders No 93. The Company will move into the LINE on 8-1-19. Moving into Rest billets at HUMBERCAMPS. Move to be completed by 3 p.m 8-1-19.			
2.	Section No.	Gun No.	No. in Line and Position of Gun in Line.	No. of Section Relieving.	No. of Gun Relieving.
	Coy HD QRS		Parade at		
	No 1 Section		11-30 a.m March in Company column of Route to		
	No 2 Section		CROSS ROADS 500x W of SOLERNEAU (Sq 9.4) From that Point. move by Sections at 150x distance (Coy HD Qrs leading)		
	No 3 Section		Via. GAUDIEMPRE to HUMBERCAMPS.		
	No 4 Section				
	BILLETING PARTY		Meet leading Section at CROSS ROADS N.W of HUMBERCAMPS.		

F. J. Hartley Lt & Adjt
199. M.G. Coy.

Vol 3

SECRET.

WAR DIARY.

OF

199th Machine Gun Company

FOR

February 1917.

WAR DIARY / INTELLIGENCE SUMMARY

Army Form C. 2118.

PAGE NO 11

of No 199. MACHINE GUN COMPANY

For FEBRUARY 1917.

Place	Date	Hour	Summary of Events and Information	Remarks and references to Appendices
HUMBERCAMPS	20/1/17		Weather cold, frost continues, snow during day. A cloudy day. A quiet day in Billet area. Artillery quiet. Company Route March during forenoon. Lewis and Stokes gun detachments. Men made dump fatigues continued. Lindsey & Co. left & lent sections to Beaumont. O.C. 16 Division. 2/Lt BARKER & 9 other Ranks returned from Trenches. Rifle section at 1 pm proceeding to relieve section on A.A work. Convoi. Pte NEWTON wounded by shell. Trenches lent section Pte PARK & Tuck to R.A. ascertained learning situation carried off. Strength accordingly. LIEUT FISHER to Hospital from A.A. Convoi. A quiet night. Cas: 1 off. Casualties 1.O.R. wounded Strength of Company 10 Offrs 143 other Ranks (1 Offr 4 1st Aid Ambulance)	ypresent
HUMBERCAMPS	21/1/17		Weather cold, frost continues, snow during day. A quiet day in Billet area. Company on fatigues during day. Artillery quiet throughout forenoon. HARTLEY & 14 O.R. lay to ascertain. Relief. Recce returned ablt 8 at 9am carrying stores & forth. Lt to Lt. Bt. Nachok at Commds on a members of Outposts & Junction to Belt Extensions from HQ. Artillery active throughout day. Lelieve Fishers lent section at night. Strength at Company 10 Offrs. 143 O.R. Casualties Sick 0nc.	ypresent
HUMBERCAMPS	1/2/17		A very cold day, frost continued. Atmosphere bright. Patrols returned from line during day. They appear to have benefitted greatly by their rest, especially in the matter of being fully uniformed about dismounting Lt PORTER & party returned from A.A. work at LAPUGNOIS ST QUENTIN at midday. I propose to have No. 1 Section completely trained in. Lent 2 current duties, starting them off this duties on the morrow. HARTLEY, ASQUITH, BARKER & LINDLEY to BALLEULMONT to attend lectures on Gunnery duties. Quick good letters. They benefitted greatly. Our Artillery quite active throughout day. Also No.2 coys mighty hasle guns turned Mules & Camp for several hours it was a deratting artillery shelling, but Camp to matinee damage. Inspected Mule lines with a view to their improvement. Sect. Nr.2 Casualties Ni., Strength of Company 10 Offrs 143 Oth Ranks (1 Offrs field Ambulance) Officers of Company on 1st CAPTAIN J. MUNRIE Commdy Coy. LIEUT R.J. HARTLEY R/n Command. " 5. ASQUITH No 2 Section Commdt " E.W. PORTER " 1 " " E.J. FISHER Sect (Brev) & LIEUT A.C. LINDLEY No 4 Section Commdt " D.B. ADAM " 3 " " " W.P. BARKER " 2 " " Sub Sect Command. " R. ELSON " 4 " " -do- " W.F. Thanks Trans. Offr. & adjut Med.	ypresent

2449 Wt. W14957/M90 750,000 1/16 J.B.C. & A. Forms/C.2118/12.

WAR DIARY / INTELLIGENCE SUMMARY

Army Form C. 2118.

Of No. 199. MACHINE GUN COMPANY.

for FEBRUARY. 1914.

PAGE No. 12.

Place	Date	Hour	Summary of Events and Information	Remarks and references to Appendices
HUMBERCAMPS	2/2/14		Bright day. Frost continues. Atmosphere fine. Aeroplanes active during forenoon. No 1 Section commanded Anti Aircraft training as section is considered at least to strike the all other duties to divert them. Complete as a section. Intended that they would be ready at sufficient France in 10 days time. Party of 20 men under W LINDLEY & LABRET unloading stores etc. Work from 8.30am to 4pm. Adjutant informed that LIEUT/FISHER had gone to Base Hospital. Pte JONES 33 Bn No 6 Station situated Inf Brigade relief on Route & proceeds to hypt 9pm. Attention to distribution of Billets. Company remains Stationary. Improvements Carried out. Movements of Billet 1st village. Captain & Party active throughout day. A very quiet night. SUPP! Casualties nil. Strength of Company 10 officers 142 others Ranks. (1 officer & Base Hospital.)	[signature]
HUMBERCAMPS	3/2/14		Weather cold, although bright, frost continues. No 1 Section continued Anti Aircraft training. We ensured 60 men to GAUDIEMPRE for Pontoon Party under THE Coy P.E. from 8am to 4pm. L/HARTLEY & HDQ 11,12 & 14 Bde to Pontoon Attachment Power for Instruction. W PHIPPS to LAPE for Clothes. Lt Col LOCKE to S.O. appointed Corp M.S.O. XVIII Corps. Coy took the chain I've checked E. Anti Aircraft Gun Mountings when enabling No 1 Section to carry on with this practice plant in training. Three Mountings, it's understood at not available for the work, improvements have been suggested that's undergoing steps at Billets and Artillery active throughout the day. Different shell burst this late Route. A quiet day in village of Billets. Gun man from trenches developed of the Company with much leakage after their tour of duty in the trenches. Cost enough in hand at most, care enough in time & event. (1 officer at Base.) Reported of broken left foot. Has no reward nil. 9 it. Strength of Company 10 off. 142 other Ranks. (1 officer Base). A quiet night. Casualties nil.	[signature]
HUMBERCAMPS	4/2/14		Weather cold. Frost continues. Atmosphere bright & dry. Bright garden of N.E. at 6am to Trenches attached to 11 of 14 Bde. M.G. Coy. No 1 Section continues AA. Training. Aeroplanes very good. Remainder of Company. Route March. Commenced. W HARTLEY & GAVINCOURT for Cash. Patch Company out during afternoon. Building of a shed for storage of Mule lines. Strength of Company 100ff 142 other Ranks. (1 off, Base). A quiet day in Billets. Night quiet. Sect Nil. Casualties Nil.	[signature]
HUMBERCAMPS	5/2/14		Another cold day. Freezing day & night. Aeroplanes full during forenoon. Vicinity of Village shelled during early hours of the morning. No Casualties little. No 1 Section continued AA instruction. Remainder of Company sent work during forenoon, during still afternoon 2 gave them a lecture on Trench Raiding. Object to this Lecture out, possible staff during the winter months than by necessary in order to thoroughly inoculate into the minds of the Machine Gunner, the important of every man's work so as to be called upon to take both in the preparation & the execution of a French Raid, & how to handle a hostile raid. A quiet day in village the Billets of the hub. Casualties Nil. Strength of Company remains excellent in spite of the severe W ASQUITH Sect on Billet. Pte B&R Nil. 10 off 142 other Rank. (1 off. Base).	[signature]

2449 Wt. W14957/Mgo 750,000 1/16 J.B.C. & A. Forms/C.2118/12.

Army Form C. 2118.

Page No. 1D.

Instructions regarding War Diaries and Intelligence Summaries are contained in F.S. Regs., Part II. and the Staff Manual respectively. Title Pages will be prepared in manuscript.

WAR DIARY
or
INTELLIGENCE SUMMARY

of No. 199, MACHINE GUN COMPANY.

for FEBRUARY 1914

(Erase heading not required.)

Place	Date	Hour	Summary of Events and Information	Remarks and references to Appendices
HUMBERCAMPS	6/2/14		A cold day still freezing. Atmosphere foggy. No 1 Section continues A.A. training. Guns of No 4 Section to Divisional Armourer Shop Capt LA GAUCHIE for overhauling. Remainder of company Route March during forenoon. Lecture on French fear Provision & cuts during afternoon. Lt HARLEY & L/SON to 1148 Bty. lately recruiting. They returned at 5 p.m. A quiet day in Village & Billets. Lt ASQUITH sick — Billet. Pt MARKS to Field Ambulance. Sick Our artillery active throughout day & night. Aerial activity during forenoon, otherwise a quiet day. Sick 2. Cadzaville. M.d. Strength of Company 100 Off: 142 3 other Ranks. (1 Off. Basrtos, 1 O.R. Field Amb)	Absent
HUMBERCAMPS	7/2/14		A fair day, clear, warmer night & day. Whole Company engaged on Morning Parties No 3 & 5 dummy attack. Visitors Lt Q.R & Col R.E to D.H.Q. to Bde Ring, the Q.M/Sector to reconnoitre & link Lt ASQUITH with a Billet. No 4 Section Gun-bath from Div. Armourer after heading two men (Pt SCARBS, accidentally injured with a falling axe whilst attic felling) Admitted to Field Ambulance. Pt ARCHER, also to Field Ambulance Sick. Louse of Pt SCARB unreadable at journalist. A quiet day in Billets & Village. Aerial activity throughout forenoon. Artillery activity throughout day & night. Sick 2. Cadzaville. M.d. Strength of Company 100 Off: 142 3 other Ranks (1 Off. Base Hos, 3 O.R. F.Amb.	Absent
HUMBERCAMPS	8/2/14		A fine day, atmosphere bright. Aeroplane activity throughout forenoon. Artillery activity throughout day. No 2 Section limbs to Bn's Ammunition Shop for overhauling. Of hole Company on Bus through Scott and Gamgown lectures, O/Rkm/6 facilities for attn & Practical demonstrations. Pole mounting Drill Medically inspected for Rein-forcements to suspected cases of scabies found at Isolated. A quiet day in Billets & village. Lt HARLEY & to Bay-NECOURT to see about washing. Lt ASQUITH is likely from Sick List, & member of the men have broken out into scabies, but Medical Officer cleft that it is nothing serious. Otherwise they all, clean & healthy. 9 put it down to the change in their way of living the snack they arrived in the company. Sgt HILL to Field Ambulance. A youn might in Rullet & Village. Cadzaville M.d. Strength 100 Off: 142 other Ranks. (1 Off. Base Hos. 4 O.R. Field Ambulance)	Absent
HUMBERCAMPS	9/2/14		A fine day, rather cold. Almost left fough. Aerial activity during forenoon, Artillery activity throughout day. A quiet day in Village & Vicinity. HARLEY to BAVINCOURT for orderly Officer are conference of officers. Company engaged on fatigues, Completed removal of manure from lines. Pte WILTSHIRE was this day accidentally wounded in the foot, through the carelessness of an infantry Party, leaving a loaded rifle in charge, their bullet & unexploded cartridge being thrown into it. The injury was not serious, but necessitated this removal to Field Ambulance. No 1 Section examined on the conclusion of its invited Anti Aircraft work. Results satisfactory, they have evidently taken great interest in this work. Six of suspected cases of scabies were sent to Field Ambulance. Otherwise all. Artillery active during night Strength of Company 10 Off: 143 other Ranks. (1 Off Base Hos. 9 O. R. Field Ambulance)	Absent

2449 Wt. W14957/M90 750,000 1/16 J.B.C. & A. Forms/C.2118/12.

WAR DIARY or INTELLIGENCE SUMMARY

Army Form C. 2118.

PAGE No. 14.

No. 199. MACHINE GUN COMPANY

for FEBRUARY 1919.

Place	Date	Hour	Summary of Events and Information	Remarks and references to Appendices
HUMBERCAMP	10/2/19		A fine day, slightly warm. Atmosphere bright. Aerial activity & artillery activity throughout the day throughout. Company on fatigue during forenoon. Company to Baths during afternoon. No 3 Section returned from Inds. Command after breakfast. O.C. Coy to B/Hd. Asquith, Blunden's attended lecture on Court Martial. O.C. Coy to Bn Hd. Qrs re report progress made in O. & W. of R. System & St MARKS to Bn Regt Stn. (Pt Hemsley & 1st Ad Ambulants (S&R), St MARKS attached to duty from D.R.S. to HARTLEY & HANNESCAMPS to 1/Wilts Read the condition of the New War Loan to the company & explained its advantages etc. Artillery active throughout night. Strength of Company 10 Off 148 Other Ranks (10ff 138nk) (po.Rto.)	[signature]
HUMBERCAMP	11/2/19		A fine day fairly warm. Aerial activity throughout day. Company engaged on wiring parties throughout day. Pt Smith 3 to No 1 field hosp. Coy Sgt & Stn On Battalion action Machine & Sect Officers Capt to Platheads to meet me informed walked there until midnight. Two other storms up returned to Billets. During the forenoon Bullets were walked by the BAATOMA 49 Divl. Hauled out except mounting over to Brigade Companies in the Thorougfure Line of Bullets of March. 49 B of each, to become Billets in Reserve point. Am of Officers they should not be used in front line Trenches owing to the chance of them being destroyed by hostile shelling. Trench Relief carried out by 114 & Bring during night. Artillery activity throughout day & night. Sick Pte H. Bean (Cr.H.) 14... Strength of Coy 10Off. 142 o/Rks (10ff.138nks 9.6.R A)	[signature]
HUMBERCAMP	12/2/19		A mild day, dull overcast, slight snow at night. Artillery rather quiet during day. Reinforcements arrived. 1 Officer & 1 N.C.O. (E.W. Thomas & Pte Tome). Both posted to No 1 Section. Company Limits packed & cleaning during forenoon. Section officers during afternoon. Made enquiries re washing by Civilians re-outfits. A quiet day in Village & Billets. Artillery active throughout night. Lectures. Transport during forenoon. Troops taken to Motor M.V. Lecture & shower room. Example of neglect of horses (Pte Steemsey Rn 4.1 & C.C.S. & Pte Archer & ovulation to No1 Rest Station & Cavalier 1 B.R & C.C.S. Strength of Company 11 Off (138nks) 143. Other Ranks. (4 FieldsAmb. 1st B.R.S.)	[signature]
HUMBERCAMP	13/2/19		A mild day. Bright. & has commenced. Company engaged on working parties throughout day. 1st Section bathed during afternoon of No 2 Section gone to Bn Command first bath during. Artillery active throughout forenoon. HARTLEY & BARNIE & H.ADAM & PORTER to Pas dimensions duties Quiet in Village & Billets during forenoon. Watercart to BRIEULL GROTTARD for reports, burst pipe on account of frost. HARTLEY & St POL on Sanitation course during afternoon. LMSQ with 1st PTE Report burst pipe on account of frost. HARTLEY & St POL on Sanitation course during afternoon. L.A.S.Q with 1st PTE VIOLET ARTILLERY 1/16. Bh. Command. Company paid out during afternoon. Pte WILTSHIRE to duty from D.R.S. Violet Artillery activity during night. Pte H.T. Bean next to horse Lines collapsed about 6.30 p.m. Pte Watson escaped from injury by Mobles. Placed under arrest for shooting of work. Casualties. NL Strength 11 off (138nk) 148 o/Rks. (4 Ad. Ambulance).	[signature]

WAR DIARY
INTELLIGENCE SUMMARY
of No. 109. MACHINE GUN COMPANY.
for FEBRUARY 1914.

Army Form C. 2118.

Place	Date	Hour	Summary of Events and Information	Remarks and references to Appendices
HUMBERCAMPS	14/2/14		A mild day; cold wind at intervals. Arile activity during forenoon. A the action throughout day. Company working parties during forenoon. Medical inspection during afternoon. Inspected carts & leckie. Camp ek. Batchelor. A quiet day in village & vicinity. No 1 Section train to Div. H.Q. for overhauling. Artillery active throughout night. Sick Amb. to amlet. N. R. Personnel returned from Trenches. Strength of Comp. any 11 Offr. (15 Sarnt) 142 Other Ranks. (L.G. +A)	[illeg]
HUMBERCAMPS	15/2/14		A mild day, bright. Aerial activity throughout day. Artillery activity throughout day. Company working parties. N/Acquit to Bn. Sgd of PAVINCOURT to see about disinfecting of Hatkot. N/A Elton & Barner with working parties. Quiet day in Village & Bulk. Game of Section returned to its cannon. Report duty again now Fridays gone off. Ge Hash to P.A. Leckie. Suspected Other Ger R. B. Artillery party active throughout night. Sick 2 Casualties (N.L. L. E. Waro the Hoxton from I.A. duty. Strength of Coy. 11 Offr. (15 Sarnt) 142 O. Ranks (5 Field Amb.	[illeg]
HUMBERCAMPS	16/2/14		Cold & freezing during forenoon. Thaw & slight rain during afternoon. Artillery faint action throughout day & night. A few small shells fell in vicinity of Village during day. No flashag; some Company in fatigue & working parties throughout day. Pt Ranos from field amb. to duty. Sick R.B. 16 casualties. N.L. Strength of Coy. 11 Offr. (1 Sarnt) 142 O. Ranks (4 Field Ambulance)	[illeg]
HUMBERCAMPS	17/2/14		A mild forenoon mostly. Cold favoured evening of rain. Company ground working parties & fatigues during day. O.E. Cay & Sasquith to Bn. H.Q. to see about de Mounting 3 officer units to show Hir dis it served a quiet day in village & Culick. Artillery very quiet. Sent 3 Other Ranks to Field Ambulance. To consolation N. pt Archer to Rankin from B.T.S. Receives Bn. Operation orders No 9b. the division being relieved by the 58th Division. A quiet night. Artillery quiet. Strength of Company 11 Officers, 142 Other Ranks (1 officer Back & 10 other Ranks field Ambulance.)	[illeg]
HUMBERCAMPS	18/2/14		A mild day, slowly thoroughly wet in dirty underfoot. Company attended Brigade lecture during forenoon. Quiet in Village & Culick. Artillery slackin during day & night. N. Lindey & Thomas to Amb. Lay to reconnoitre Sector O.E. Coy to Squaspk to attend lecture on offensive gas operations. Pt Whitehorn to Field ambulance. Sick O.E. Coy to Bn. W.Gs during evening to discuss order concerning Recent Reinforcement of 3 Machine Sumners from Brook. also 3 high drafts Hostio to complete establishment of animals. Strength of Coy. 11 Offr. (1 Sarnt) 145 Other Ranks (1 Offr. Back & amb.)	[illeg]
HUMBERCAMPS	19/2/14		A mild day. Show continues, roads slushy Day dull & overcast Company found work Rmg. parties throughout day. Lt Harvey returned from S/T Pop. O.E. Coy & H.Q. Gr, Imb, W.T. & 118 Pod & also 142 Other Ranks (14) Army. M. Cay. to attend on ordinates. Ne Crick (rescuth Mornituca). Qt Nash returned from field amb. pt Macoms & Lya Coy in Ballieulmont. Sick H.G. Causelties N.L. Strength of Company 11 Offr. (1 Sarnt) 145 Other Ranks (1 e 6 cas amb.)	[illeg]

PAGE No. 10

Army Form C. 2118.

WAR DIARY
or
INTELLIGENCE SUMMARY

of No 199 MACHINE GUN COMPANY

4th FEBRUARY 1917

Place	Date	Hour	Summary of Events and Information	Remarks and references to Appendices
BUMBERCAMPS	20/2/17		A mild day. Rain all day. Company found Working Parties during day. O.C. Coy to Bn Hd Qrs during forenoon, then on to 146 Bn & Coy headquarters to see about relief by 98 Coy. Quiet day on Bullets & vicinity. Artillery, trench mortar, towards evening. SL & M.L Baronettes fired. No Bn Hd Qrs during evening re Anti-Aircraft M.G.s. No casualties. M.G.Coy detaining move to 1st Army. Strength of Coy: 11 offr (1 Baoo) 145 other Ranks. (16 Field Ambulances). Operation orders M.G.Coy detaining move to 1st Army. Strength of Coy: 11 offr (1 Baoo) 145 other Ranks. (16 Field Ambulances).	Appx 1
BUMBERCAMPS	21/2/17		A mild day. Cloudy & overcast. Company engaged on Working Parties & fatigues during day. Artillery fairly quiet during day & night. Quiet day in Bullets & vicinity. 2nd Lts PORTER & ADAM to tap station for reporting in BAILLEULMONT to see 196 M.G. Coy re tofting over from 146 Coy. 2nd Lt 16 Bn Hd Qrs during evening re Anti-Aircraft positions. Sent E. BROWN to H.A. But to Sulatin Field. Strength of Coy: 11 offr (1 Baoo) 145 other R.Rs. (8 Batt. Amb.)	Appx 2
BUMBERCAMPS	22/2/17		A mild day, cloudy & overcast. Company on Route March to HARTLEY & PAS on reconnaissance. Self & Pioneer 2nd Lts HART & RIAL M.G.CA. & then 2nd Lts MASON & SUMMOND on Route M. Most Parades quite a good condition. Sgt HILL & Pt. PACKWELL returned from Field Ambulance. Pt. PRATNER to Field Amt. 3 N.C.O's returned from Inf Gas School. Quiet day in village & Bullets. Gas Alarm during night. Artillery active throughout day, quiet action during night. SL & Over Baoulette Strength of Coy: 11 offr (1 Baoo) 145 other Ranks (4 Field Ambulance).	Appx 3
BUMBERCAMPS	23/2/17		A mild day, dull & overcast. Company on Route March during afternoon. AT HARTLEYS Major to see about G.S. wagon. Artillery active throughout day. Quiet day in village & vicinity. Sgt POLLARD to Field Amt. Men marched very well during Route March, whilst was done in full marching order. distance 12 miles. Self to Amath. Field. Strength of Coy: 11 offr 145 other R.Rs. (8 Field Ambt), 1 offr Paris.	Appx 4
BUMBERCAMPS	24/2/17		A mild, dull, cloudy & overcast, bad day for any observation. Company to P.o.W. during forenoon, heavy batteries during afternoon. A quiet day in village & vicinity. Artillery fairly active throughout day & night. Lt HARTLEY & C.O.S during afternoon. Paid Company out during afternoon. 2 Lts PSH & BULL Amt. Sert BF BUCKley from the Amt. during night received news from Divvery Paid. Third day for front of 5th Corps.(S) 2 men of 14th (RES) 145 OR. (8 Field Ambulance) ready to move at short notice. JCM I Baon Mr. M.I. Strength of Coy: 11 offr (1 Baon) 145 O.Rs (8 Field Ambulance)	Appx 5
BUMBERCAMPS	25/2/17		A mild day, dull & overcast. Company ready to move at 5 a.m. O.R 10.16. Received message cancelling move's at about 10.15. Body cheer cleaning up Camp & Quarters previous to vacating camp on next day. Company operation orders No.2 issued. A quiet day in village & Bullets. Artillery active throughout day. Sgt BYRNE & Men to B.A.R. or O.P. of at. A. Strength of Company 11 offr (8 Ns) 145 O.R. O.P. 4t. A.	Appx 6

Army Form C. 2118.

WAR DIARY
INTELLIGENCE SUMMARY of N° 199. MACHINE GUN COMPANY

for FEBRUARY 1914

PAGE N° 14

Place	Date	Hour	Summary of Events and Information	Remarks and references to Appendices
HUMBERCAMPS	26/2/14		A fine day, rather dull. In accordance with 191 Operation orders the Company left HUMBERCAMPS for BOCQUEMAISON via COUTURELLE. Parades & Marched off at 9.45 a.m. Turnout of Company good. Transport very good. Route on a bad roads made marching very heavy. Several long delays owing to much Mud. Several Motor Lorries, on which occasion had to get to the front, heavy night for Limbers start good example of outspank of draught horse and mules. Mid day halt at HUMBERCOURT, where watered & fed. Reached BOCQUEMAISON at 11.15 p.m. Mess Lt HARVEY & Buck. Partÿ. Billets completed by 5 pm. A quiet night. No Casualties. Strength of Company 11 Offs (1 Bank) 145 other Ranks (9 Excess Audt) The move from HUMBERCAMPS Completes the Camp Stay. 1st Level of duty in the Line. The Condition during the period was alright. Such below normal, & the experience gained by the personnel of the unit most invaluable. Arrived at BOCQUE MAISON reported to 1148th Inf Brigade under whose orders we now march.	[signature]

In the field
21-2-14

[signature]
Commdg 199 Machine Gun Coy

Copy No. 2.

Coy Form 1.

No. 199 MACHINE GUN COMPANY.

OPERATION ORDERS. No. 2 By
CAPTAIN. J. MUHLIG. M.C. Commanding 199 M.G. Coy.

At HUMBERCAMPS.   Dated 25-2-17.

REFERENCE MAP. LENS. 11. 1/40000

1. In conjunction with H.Q⁺⁺ Division Operation Order N° 97. the Company will leave HUMBERCAMP on 26ᵗʰ inst. for LE SOUICH AREA arriving same date at Billeting under orders of 148ᵗʰ Iny Brigade at BOUQUE MAISON. Route via COULEREUVE.

2.

Section No.	Gun No.	No. in Line and Position of Gun in Line.	No. of Section Relieving.	No. of Gun Relieving.
N° 1 Section		Parade at 9-10 am.	Sections will march	
N° 2 —"—		Move off at 9.30 am. N° 1 Section Leading.	at 200ˣ distances between Sections until WEST of ARRAS-DOULLENS ROAD.	
N° 3 —"—				
N° 4 —"—				
Coy Hd Qrs		Ammunition Limbers will accompany Sections.		
Billeting Party		Lt HARTLEY & 3 other Ranks. Parade with Bicycles under orders from Lt HARTLEY	To Report to Town MAJOR BOUQUE MAISON on Morning 26ᵗʰ inst	

25-2-17
Copies N° 1 to Office
N° 2 to Diary

R. Hartley Lt & Adjt
199 Machine Gun Company

OPERATION ORDERS—continued Sheet No. 2.

3.

PARADE. The Company will parade in Marching order, Steel Helmets at 9-10 am.

4 BLANKETS. Will be rolled by Sections & Stacked by opposite Grooms Billets by 9 am.

5 BILLETS. Will be thoroughly cleaned out, & all straw & refuse taken to incinerator by 8-15 am.

6 FATIGUES.
1 N.C.O & 12 men for loading LORRY at 8 am.
1 N.C.O & 4   "   "   Officers Mess at 8 am.
1 N.C.O & 8   "   "   Engine Shed, Incinerator & Latrines at 8-30 am.

7 Billeting Party. Lt HARTLEY. Sgt HEATH, Cpl BATES, Pte TYRRELL.

8 Officers Kits. To be at Grooms Billets by 8 am.

9 TRANSPORT. Drivers Packs, Rugs etc. to be on their respective limbers before 8 am. NO DRIVERS KIT WILL BE accepted after that hour.

10 RATIONS.
A haversack ration will be carried.
Full feeds to be carried.
Spare Rations & Forage. to be at Grooms Billet by 4-30 am.

11 ROUTINE.
Reveille   6. A.M.
Breakfast 6-30 A.M.

12 INSPECTION. Inspection of Camp & Mule Lines at 8-45 am.

13 GENERAL. All Cooks gear & A.M. Stores will go by Motor Lorry, accompanied by A/M Sgt, Cooks & L/C Osborne.
In the event of No. Lorry being available. Cooks will take Spare Rations & Cooks gear on Cooks Cart also & carts.
(Add Officers Mess & L/C Jackett.) Billeting Party. also Cpl LANCASTER.
Blankets, Leather Jerkins, Horse Rugs will go on H.S. Wagon.

14 Departure. Lorry leaves Billets at 8-30 am.

15 Inspection:- Section Commdrs will inspect their Sections before marching of saddlery, condition & Packing of valises & Waterproof Sheets.

25.2.19.

Act. Adjt.
M. G. Company.

No. 199.

OPERATION ORDERS—continued   Sheet No. **2**.

3. PARADE. Coy will parade in Marching Order. Steel Helmets on. Canteens without covers will not be showing outside Valises.

4. BLANKETS. Will be rolled by Sections & Stacked in Q.M. Stores by 6.30 am

5. JERKINS. Will be neatly placed in the Fighting Limbers by 6.30 am

6. HORSE RUGS. Will be packed in N° 3. Limbers by 6 am. (also drivers Packs)

7. BIVOUACS & LINES. Will be thoroughly cleaned & ready for inspection at Latrines filled in by 4 am

8. Burial Party. Lt HARTLEY. Sgt HEATH. Cpl. BATES. Pte Pinnock

9. Officers Kits. To be at Qr Ms Stores at 4 am

10. RATIONS. A haversack ration will be carried.
    Full Feeds to be carried.
    Spare Rations & Forage to be at Qr Ms Stores by 6.30 am

11. ROUTINE. Reveille 5 A.M.
    Breakfast 5.30 am

12. MOTOR TRANSPORT. A Motor Lorry will call at the Qr Ms Stores at about 11 am. & will take Blankets, Stores, etc. not carried on 1st Line Transport to destination. (add damaged Bicycles) Party to accompany Lorry. C.Q.M.Sgt BALKWELL, Pte WHITEHORN Pte ~~Moss Welles~~ Foxlee, Smith. (Lt Barker in charge.

13. General. Cooks to accompany Cooks Cart.
    Officers Mess & Cooks Gear to go on Mess Cart.
    Water Cart to be filled
    The Men remaining under Lt Barker will clean up generally after the departure of the Coy

                                            Act. Adjt.
                                            M. G. Company.

Copies N° 1. to Officer
  "   " 2 " Diary

Copy No. 2.

1

Coy Form 1

No. 199 MACHINE GUN COMPANY.

OPERATION ORDERS. No. 3. By
CAPTAIN J. MUHLIG. M.C.
Commanding 199 M.G. Coy.

At BOUQUÉ MAISON. Dated 28-2-17.

REFERENCE MAP. LENS 1/100000

1. In accordance with 148 IB O.O. No 113 the Coy will move to HERMICOURT via FREVONT on 1-3-17. Billeting at HERDICOURT.

2.	Section No.	Gun No.	No. in Line and Position of Gun in Line	No. of Section Relieving.	No. of Gun Relieving.
	No 1		Parade at	Transport	
	No 2		7.40. a.m.	in	
	No 3		Move off in Column of Route	Rear of	
	No 4		No 2 Section Leading.	Column.	
	Coy Hd Qrs		followed by No 3, No 4, Coy Hd Qrs, N.I.	Ammn Limb Grouped in	
	Billeting Party.		Lt HARTLEY & 3 other Ranks Parade with Bicycles under the orders of Lt Hartley.	Rear of Lighters.	

Copies No 1. to Officer
"   " 2 " "

R.J. Hartley Lt & A/Adjt
199 M.G. Coy

OPERATION ORDERS—continued   Sheet No. **2**.

3. PARADE:— Coy will parade in Marching Order at. 9.45 a.m.

4. BLANKETS. Will be rolled by Sections & stacked in Stores. 9 a.m.

5. JERKINS. Will be placed in Fighting Limbers.

6. HORSE RUGS. Will be packed in No. 3. Limbers.

7. BILLETS. Will be left clean & latrines filled in. Inspection of lines to be before marching off.

8. BILLETING PARTY. Lt. HARTLEY, Sgt. HEATH. Cpl. BATES.

9. Representative to draw Rations. Cpl. LANCASTER. To be at . . . . . . by 8 a.m.

10. Officers Kits. To be in Stores by 9 a.m.

11. RATIONS. HAVERSACK Ration will be carried. Nose feeds on Animals, & Haynets on Limbers. Spare Rations & Forage to Stores for Motor Transport.

12. ROUTINE. Reveille 6 a.m. Breakfast 6.45 a.m.

13. MOTOR TRANSPORT. Under Lt. BARKER. Orders will be issued later. To accompany lorries CQMS BALKWELL, Pte FOXLEE, SMITH, EVISON,

14. General. Cooks to accompany Cooks Cart. Offrs Mess & Cooks Gear to go in Cooks Cart. Water Cart to be filled. Limbers Greased before Moving off. The lorry party will clean up Billets after.

15. STEEL HELMETS. Must be cleaned, with oil if necessary.

                                                     R. Lindley Major.
                                                           Act. Adjt.
                                                      M. G. Company.

SECRET.

WAR DIARY.

OF

109th Machine Gun Company

FOR

March 1917.

WAR DIARY

of **N° 199 MACHINE GUN COMPANY**

INTELLIGENCE SUMMARY

1st MARCH 1917

Army Form C. 2118.

Page N°. 18.

Place	Date	Hour	Summary of Events and Information	Remarks and references to Appendices
BOUQUEMAISON	24/2/17		A fine day. Warm + Bright. Company spent day cleaning up + repacking limbers etc. after previous days march. Visited by G.O.C. division during afternoon. Received 11th Bgd. Operation order N° 112 which did not effect the Company. Allotted to or shall in a lorry fetching rations. Overlanded others + joined others to cut down a little. Billets in BOUQUEMAISON very good. Rest company has occupied since its arrival in the country. During afternoon received 1st reinforcements from Base (in Michelin Gunner) POSTED as follows 15 M.O.S.(Est) N°.2 + 2 to 4th Section. all of good physique + apt to stand work. Cpl BURDEN to Field Ambulance (sick). A quiet uneventful day & night. Casualties NIL. Strength of Bgd. 11 Off. (1 Baud.) 149 Other Ranks (8. O.R. Field Amb.)	[initials]
BOUQUEMAISON	25/2/17		A dull day, rather cold + overcast. Company on fatigue drill, chem. cleaning up in afternoon. 4th Bgd. arrived in village. O.C. + Asquith to BONNIÈRES re O.C. 11th B.M.G. Coy. at Much Lorry arms 32 miles logged during the day. Res LAVERN + WHITEHORN to duty from Field Ambulance. Bonville 205. Sgt Rlee. Str. of the Strength of Coy. 11 Off. (1 Baud.) 149 Other Ranks (6 Field Amb.) Operation Orders 11th B. Bgy N° 113 received. Coy. Spent Sunday. N°3 rested. (Copies attached)	[initials]
BOUQUEMAISON en route to HERMICOURT	1/3/17		A dull morning, rather cold, but got warmer during day. Paraded + left BOUQUEMAISON for HERMICOURT via FREVENT + St POL. by Route March. Marching in conjunction with 11th B Bgy orders N°113. Followed near of 11th Bgy R.E. at present marched past G.O.C. the division. After a tiring day reached HERMICOURT at 4.30p.m. Casualties en route. Men marched well. Lt BARNES left with lorry at 12 noon + arrived an Billets with loads. Billets good. Col. BATES to Bony Hd. Qrs. at CROIX with arrival reports. Lonville NID + Pentilhem. returned. Drove Qrs. to L.A. Strength of Company 11 Off. 149 Other Ranks (4 Field Amb.)	[initials]
HERMICOURT en route AUMERVAL	2/3/17		A cold misty morning, got warmer during day. In conjunction with 11th B.J.B. operation orders N° 114 paraded + left HERMICOURT for AUMERVAL. marched in 5th Column under command of Major Chambers of B. H.Q. 4th Coy. Route via St POL, + PERNES. Arrived in AUMERVAL at 3-30p.m. saw HARTLEY + found billets arranged. Company marched rather well + arrived without casualties. LINDSEY saw dock on arrival, a few mens soft feet which were speedily attended to. Received 11th Bgy. O. Order N° 115 + issued Coy. ord. orde N°5. All had a good nights rest, getting to sleep quiet early. A quiet night, all orders received + carried by 10p.m. No more other N.C. Strength of Bgd. 11 Off. (1 Baud.) 149 Other Ranks (4 Field Ambulance.	[initials]

WAR DIARY or **INTELLIGENCE SUMMARY**

Army Form C. 2118.

of N°. 199 MACHINE GUN COMPANY.

for MARCH 1914.

Page N°. 19.

Place	Date	Hour	Summary of Events and Information	Remarks and references to Appendices
AUMERVAL en Route HAVERSKIRQUE	2/3/14		A cold, misty morning. In conjunction with N°8 & 3 Operation order N°15, 199 Company proceeded to HAVERSKIRQUE by Route March, left AUMERVAL at 11.15 am. Arrived starting Point, at M-noon. had lunch & proceeded party first at 12.15 pm, marching on Rear of M&T.M. Battery. Proceeded via Lillers & Busnes & Gr. Vevant to Billets. Arrived at 5.15 pm. Owing to after leaving Lillers Hot. Generale, there being no arrangement for men up to date, they arrived thoroughly tired (no casualties en Route). Recruit Minor Cases of little feet seen to by Lt-HINDEY on arrival in Billets. Billets good. A quiet night. Sick Nil. Casualties Nil. Strength of Company 11 offr. (1 Batt. Hq.) 149 other Ranks. (4 Field Ambulance)	[signature]
HAVERSKIRQUE en Route LA GRAND PACAUT	4/3/14		A fine day, bright & mild. In conjunction with 148 Inf Bang Operation orders N°116 Company proceeded by Route March to the GRAND PACAUT, a suburb of MERVILLE. Company marched via CALONNE Sur by L/S. under Lt. ELSON. O.C. Coy & Lt Section Bombards by Motr. lorrey with other officers of 148 G.C.O. to join line HAVERTIE AREA. On arrival at LAVENTIE found R.H. Coy of 56th Bn was 193 M.G. Coy. Capt RAMSEY on Command. Section officers visited Trenches of Division. Company arrived in Billets at Le GRAND PACAUT at 3.45 pm. Billets good. Offr. Coy & Section bomards registered, billeted at the GRAND PACAUT at 6 pm. A quiet night, Sick Nil. Strength of Coy 11 offr. (1 B.H.a.) 149 O.Rks. (9.F.A.)	[signature]
LE GRAND PACAUT en Route LAVENTIE	5/3/14		A cold morning. Snow fell during forenoon. Company left Le GRAND PACAUT at 9 am for LAVENTIE to relieve 193 Bn Machine Gun Co. Company 9/0 the limbs. Arrived at 12 noon. Company had dinners. At 2 pm N°3 & 4 Section (4 Guns) to Right Pongy. N°2 Section to Left & Cents Pongade (2 guns to each Pongh). Relief carried out without incident & completed by 6 pm. N°3 & 4 Sections to Reserve Billets in Rue L'EPINETTE, LAVENTIE. Coy H.q. attacked to Suns Street (16.93). Owing to attacks of Motr lorry, limbers had to unload in LAVENTIE & proceed to Le GRAND PACAUT to fetch by stores. Oracle. Coy. kinds on return, but about the journeys Nnog with. A quiet night on Billets & Trenches. Reported Completion of Relief to Division. Sick Nil. 6 casualties. Nil. Strength of Coy. 11 offr. (1 B.H.M.) 149 O.Rks. (4 F.A.)	[signature]
LAVENTIE	6/3/14		A fine day, mild & bright. Sections in Reserve Cleaned & Repacked kit, fighting limbers. Changed in Billets & stores after departure of 193 M.G. Coy. O.C. Coy & Lt ADAM to Left & Centre Pongeade Sections. Visited Sections & HQrs at all guns. Journal Commencement good except for want in Roof of gunfire. Returned to Hd Qrs at 3 pm. A quiet night on Trenches & Billets. Sick Nil. 6 casualties Nil. Strength of Coy. 11 offr. (1 B.H.M.) 149 other Rks. (4 F.A.)	[signature]

WAR DIARY / INTELLIGENCE SUMMARY

PAGE No. 20.

of No. 199. MACHINE GUN COMPANY

for MARCH 1914

Army Form C. 2118.

Place	Date	Hour	Summary of Events and Information	Remarks and references to Appendices
LAVENTIE	7/3/14		A fine, cold day. Windy. Sections on Resort Billet Cleaning & Repairing Limbers during forenoon. Baths during afternoon. O.C. Coy & Right Party lector to visit N° 1 Section. Visited Section 10.15 am. & all well. New Reon & Dugout held. Sound center etc. clean & position & guns clean. Position requires a good deal of repairs doing to them. Considering the weather of late the trenches were wonderfully dry & clean. 2 guns in left forward sector fire 1500 R.d each, on hostile C.T. to French tramway. Guns worked well. Very little retaliation. A quiet 24 hours. Very little stokes artillery shots. O.C. says the Long Hd. Gun left company to arrange details. Str. Nd. Casualties Nil. Strength of Coy. 11 Off. (1 Bach) 149 other Rks (4 Field Amb)	(present)
LAVENTIE	8/3/14		A cold day. Snow during forenoon. Sections on Resort cleaning up & improving billets during forenoon. Gun Drill during afternoon. Self to Lanroain to get maps of frontage. Made up shortage. Received long defensive scheme. Lt HARTLEY to N° 1 Section to recomment report. Lt. Boy & guns from 2000 Rds each at both Front etc. Very little retaliation. Centre & Right Party Guns not yet fired, but hope to do so shortly. A quiet 24 hours. Artillery activity Normal. Pts Westaker, Irish, Coates & Evans returned from field. Received 5th Rs. reinforcement from Base (2 Machine Gunners) posted to N° 2 & 1st sections respectively. Str/B Nd. Casualties Nil. Strength of Company 11 off. (1 Bach) 181 other Rks (3 Field Amb.)	(present)
LAVENTIE	9/3/14		A cold day. Snow most of day. General activity during forenoon. Amt Ascroft & M. Lews at work, & repair one hostile glands from enlarge trenches do in compliments. Lt ADAMS & HARTLEY to ESTAIRES & SAILLY to recommend Roads & Areas. Reserve Sections engaged Re. Packing & Cleaning. Lts Sanderston & Leaventis on duty laying in Area. Artillery action Normal. Pte NORTON depart for Mudelane wrote. Strength of strength of company left & Centre Party Guns tactive fire 4000 Rds during 24 hours. wrote gun hostile R.E. area. Str Nd. Casualties Nil. Strength of Company 11 Off. (1 Bach) 180 other Rks (3 Field Amb)	(present)
LAVENTIE	10/3/14		A mild day. Bright. Officer & N.C.O. of Reserve Sections to start Trench Party to Relief O.C. inspected Billet area. Artillery activity about Normal. M. Guns busy throughout afternoon & evening. Coy of C. Ardiers (N° Essence Re. Relief. A quiet night Lt E.S. Fisher to Y.K.C. arr. 8-2-y. other Sect Nd. Deville Rd. Guns in left & Centre Party Section fire 3000 Rds on hostile bivouacs & C.T. Strength of Coy. 10 off. 180 other Rks (3 field Amb)	(present)
LAVENTIE	11/3/14		A fine day, mild & bright. General activity during forenoon. Artillery activity throughout day. M.G. activity. Relay of N° 1 & 2 sections by N° 3 & 4 sections. Complete & without hay left. A quiet day & might from except for a little artillery (hostile) fire on High Sections area. Strs Nd. Casualties Nil. Strength of Company 10 off. 180 other Rks. (3 field Amb)	(present)

WAR DIARY or INTELLIGENCE SUMMARY

Army Form C. 2118.

199 MACHINE GUN COMPANY

for March 1917

Page 21.

Place	Date	Hour	Summary of Events and Information	Remarks and references to Appendices
LAVENTIE	12/3/17		A mild day, cloudy. Rain during afternoon. Artillery active throughout day. Reserve Sections to Baths. Clean up after Relief. Return from Trenches. A quiet day. Repairs of emplacements have carried out by Sections on duty. Rifle Ping Section Rounds fired 3000 Rds on Sniper & enemy working parties. Post, otherwise quiet. Sect to No 8 relief Coys. Sect 1 Pte Crowe to title Aughatah Pte Perou to Brittain Vulgaire Casualties nil. Strength of Coy 10 Offs 180 Other Ranks. (1 of 4 will Ambulance)	Appx 1
LAVENTIE	13/3/17		A mild day, rather dull. Artillery activity throughout day. Reserve Sections Musketry instruction & sports. His Revr Col Howard Rifle Ping Section reported Shell Heavy Shrapnel Rifle Mr & T.M fire seen. Reln. Regular Sec^ns reported hostile action. O.E. Coy visited Sec^ns & Left. Parties arrive from all Sections. Trenches & ng enemy's lines improving positions. Left to Hd Qrs I/R M.G Coy saw O.C. arranged various Parades with him for 4thday instead Right Brig Sect^ns for Reserve arrived. Machine Guns in all sector active throughout the night. 4000 Rds fired on 6 hostile dumps & Belt Areas Sect NE Cassette NW. Pte Crowe to Casualty Cle Sta. Strength of Coy 10 Offs 190 OR. (3 & A)	Appx 2
LAVENTIE	14/3/17		A mild day. Night Rain at times. Reserve Sections at Games. Resv Sections "B" a Battn^n Work during afternoon. 2/Lt BARKER & 5 other Ranks of "B" Force to POSSE to be attached "B" a Battn for Consibut instruction in Anti aircraft work. In accord with C.R.O Nº 65 dtd 11-3-17. 4 horses were sent to LA BERGUE for inspecting, selected & ordered to field Depersement the same day Struck off Strength accordingly. Visited by Corps M G O (Lt Col Mullen) who saw work during transport. Full satisfactory. Scotland Corps M.G. defence scheme thought out. Gun articles busy throughout this day. During the evening outskirts of town were shelled intermittently in a very heavy gun. No damage done. Our M Guns were busy throughout the night 5000 Rds fired on hostile dumps & Sect R.N. 50 casualties old Cassette on Strength of Company 10Offs 149 Othr Rnks. (3 field Amb)	Appx 3
LAVENTIE	15/3/17		A mild day, dull. Reserve Sections at Gun Work during forenoon. Gun drill during afternoon. Gun drill during afternoon. Work sports being done by the Sections on the duty. During the 5 pm LAVENTIE was shelled by a long range gun. No damage done. A quiet night Sect at Danielle Rd Strength of Company 10 Offs 149 Other Rnks (3 & A). + 07 OR. Rds on hostile track lines.	Appx 4

WAR DIARY

INTELLIGENCE SUMMARY of 199 MACHINE GUN COMPANY

for MARCH 1914.

Army Form C. 2118.

PAGE No. 22.

Place	Date	Hour	Summary of Events and Information	Remarks and references to Appendices
LAVENTIE	16/3/14		A mild day. Fairly strong aerial activity during day. Artillery fairly active during day in turn. 4 HAMPSHIRE for fatigue for 24 hrs to see about various Gun Emplacements. All guns & Belts repeated daily. Nil report. Over 1 light strength shorts to Maidstock section. (Si&R.) Men on leave from section no 2 & 1 off to 13th Bn am. go to hosp. dump & hot baths. Ammunition expended 4000 Rds. Double operation order No 8. A quiet night. Si&R Nil. Casualties Nil. Strength of Company 10 Off 149 other Ranks (3 Field Amb)	[signature]
LAVENTIE	17/3/14		A mild day, bright, aerial activity during day, artillery both sides active throughout day. Intersection Relief carried out, No 1 & 2 sections relieve No 3 & 4 sections. Trenches respectively. Relief reported complete by 9pm. Gun from no 4 Trench no 3 & 4 section fire 1400 Rds on Working Party by 9pm. Gun from no 4 trench in German trench No Casualties. No damage done to Gun 2 sides few hits a rig. A few stoppages. Gun shells fell 45 round during thaw/thawing. 1 N.C. Clark to Field Amb Casualties Si&R 1. Field Amb Casualties Nil. Strength of Coy 10 Off 149 otR (HA)	[signature]
LAVENTIE	18/3/14		A fine day, mild & bright, aerial activity during day. 2 hostile observation balloons up over AUBERS during forenoon. Artillery active normal. Clipping of mules proceeded with. Recon section to Build & kit inspection. Guns in two expended 5000 Rds. Stowers & Gunn to Hosp Si&R 1. 1 C. Clarke to field amb. Casualties Nil. Strength of Coy 10 Off: 149 otR (5 Field amb)	[signature]
LAVENTIE	19/3/14		A fine day, cold winds. Air was strong throughout day. Recon sections guns were during relief, wild fire Guns remained within Elphin amid & wire during forenoon. Seen Nil movement on the road, whilst was fairly continuous. Say Fusilier Regt. Recon section during the afternoon found all correct & went on Emplacement going on. A quiet night. Si&R Nil. Casualties Nil. Strength of Company 10 officers 140 other Rks. 5 Field Ambulance	[signature]
LAVENTIE	20/3/14		A windy day, rain throughout day. Recon Sections at Gun Drill. Artillery activity throughout day, & few H.V. shells fell in front of Laventie post during afternoon. Hy Haufaux wirelessed Quiet. At 8.30 am wireful bombardment commenced in direction of Haufaux in direction No3 Area. Gun M.G.s busy throughout night, hold back Germans. 2nd Lt Clark to Cas C. Stn. Bohmann to arrive. Gun M.G. busy throughout night. Strong/d Coy 10 Off 148 R. (FA) Si&R 2 Nil 2.D.R to £.d. Strength of Coy 10 Off 148. R (FA)	[signature]

WAR DIARY or INTELLIGENCE SUMMARY

Army Form C. 2118.

PAGE No. 23.

of No. 199 MACHINE GUN COMPANY

for MARCH 1917

Place	Date	Hour	Summary of Events and Information	Remarks and references to Appendices
LAVENTIE	21/3/17		A cold day, bright, normal activity throughout day. M Guns on Left & Centre Bring Sectors dro'd back over hostile plank, their attempts to cross and line for a Lab. attitude. Reserve Section Medically inspected, clean bill of health. On Yet Offr inspected animals & gas clean bill of health. Clipping of mules proceeded with. Sect to Left Bring Sector to reconnoitre during evening. 10 am to Right Bring Sector during afternoon. 2 OR (Blankets disinfected under new arrangements). Artillery fairly active. A quiet 24 hrs. M.G. in line fired 250 Rds at North flank, & 2000 at hostile front wire. (Pt attempt to R.A. from Trocadero to Camellia) Nil. Strength of Coy 10 Offrs 148 other ranks. (4 Field Ambulance)	Present
LAVENTIE	22/3/17		A cold day, snow during night, bright during day, normal activity throughout day. Artillery action throughout day. Medical Inspection of Reserve Section & WH during afternoon. Inspection of animals during morning by Vet Offr. Alt offrs all ranks correct to Adm to Right Bring Sector for recon arounds At Winch & Shield and from Trocadero. O C & 15 N0.2 Section Line during night, found all correct Guns fired 5000 Rds during night. A quiet night, dark, Sick but Remd in Nil. Strength of Coy 10 Offrs 148 O.R. (4 F.A.)	Present
LAVENTIE	23/3/17		A cold day, bright. Snow during night. Recce'd Sectors to Baths during forenoon. day 15.0 e 146 enlisted go informed sky G.O.C changing disposition of guns in the line. guaues O.O.C N0S Q. Sgt A laneron to 4 Old Amb Coff N0 3 & 4 Section Relieved N0S 1 & 2 respectively in the trenches during the evening. Relief completed 9.30pm. 151 Arthingham evacuated to C.C.S. Strength of other rick N.0. Sorties Sny 10 Offrs 147 O.R. (4 F.A. sick amb) During night guns fired 4000 rds.	Present
LAVENTIE	24/3/17		A cold day, bright, normal activity throughout day. Reserve Section to Baths during forenoon. To save dull during afternoon. Artillery both sides active throughout today. During the night a violent bombardment broke out on the Left Summer Trench Camp into Days up at 11 pm during 5 days out with rank & Cartier. No M.G. fire during 24 hrs. Sgt M wounded. Bullet. Sick N.0. no mob Remd with Rank. Strength of Coy. 10 Offrs 146 O.R. (4 Field Amb)	Present

2449 (Wt. W14957/M90 750,000 1/16 J.B.C. & A. Forms/C.2118/12.

WAR DIARY or INTELLIGENCE SUMMARY

Army Form C. 2118.

PAGE 214

of No. 199 MACHINE GUN COMPANY

for MARCH 1917.

Place	Date	Hour	Summary of Events and Information	Remarks and references to Appendices
LAVENTIE	25/3/17		A mild day, bright, aerial activity during day. Artillery active throughout day & night. Reserve Sections all went in Limbers. Commenced Relief to Trench lines. Relieved orders to withdraw from Line. Self & all Beg Hd Qrs on relief of Gun Teams. Sect. No. Casualties Nil. One gun (MG Inny) throughout night Strength of Company 100 Off. 146 OR (4 field Ambulance)	present
LAVENTIE	26/3/17		A dull day, rain during day. Reserve sections to Baths during forenoon. No 3 & 4 Sections units relieved in the Trenches by their respective Army Companies & returned to Reserve Relief completed Correct by 3 pm. Lt P.E. Main returned to duty from border. Lt P. Parrott to Bn Train as detailed. A quiet day. 3rd Lieut at events HARVEY to Bn on duty He to leave for PE Simmons. Sect No. Casualties Nil. Strength of Coy 100 Off 146 OR (4 F. L.)	present
LAVENTIE	27/3/17		A cold day, snow & rain alternately during day. Company engaged cleaning up & repairing limbers & harness. Lt P.E. Arnott, & Cassells Chaney Off. Strength off strength recordingly. A quiet day & night Lt P Simmons proceeded on leave up to 4th April. Sect No. Casualties Nil. Strength of Coy 10 Off 144 other R1o (5 field amb)	present
LAVENTIE	28/3/17		A bright day, cold. Aerial activity throughout day. Artillery quite active during day. Transport went on Short Rout March during forenoon. Company to Baths during forenoon Medical Inspection during afternoon. (of other Practice during day) very good results. Sect No. Casualties Nil Strength of Coy 10 Off 144 OR (5 field Ambulance)	present
LAVENTIE	29/3/17		A wet forenoon, cleared up during afternoon. No aerial activity or artillery activity. About 10 Othe Run Lt. near Billet during forenoon a quiet night. Lt Hoskins to L Coo Chung Off. Struck off Strength. 2nd Lieut Ross Joining as such evening. Sect No. Casualties Nil Strength of Coy 10 Off 143 OR (14 fld amb)	present
LAVENTIE	30/3/17		A mild day. Quiet throughout day. Company resumed training. Patrols reconnitre Right Army Sect. A quiet night. Lt P Nelland to Bear. Struck off Strength. Sect No. Casualties Nil. Strength of Coy 100 Off 142 OR (5 Amb)	present

Murdock Capt
Commander 199 MG Coy

1   Cov Form 1.

No. 199   MACHINE GUN COMPANY.

OPERATION ORDERS.   No. 4   By

CAPTAIN J. MUHLIG

Commanding 199 M.G. Coy.

At   Dated 2-3-17

REFERENCE MAP. LENS 1/100000

1. In accordance with 148 I.B. Operation Orders No. 148 The Company will move to AUMERVALLY Route March on 2-3-17. Moving via St. Pol. Billeting at

2. Section No.	Gun No	No. in Line and Position of Gun in Line	No. of Section Relieving.	No. of Gun Relieving.
No 3		Parade at 9.15 am	Transport	
No 4		Move off in Column of Route	in Rear	
Coy Hd Qrs		No 3 heading	of	
No 1			Column	
No 2				
Billeting Party		Lt HARTLEY & 2 other Ranks Parade under orders of L/MARKS		

OPERATION ORDERS—continued Sheet No. **2**.

3. Parade: Coy Parade at   am Dress Marching order.

4. Blankets. Rolled by Sections & in Stores by 7 am

5. Jerkins Packed in Fighting Limbers.

6. Horse Rugs: Will be packed in No 3. Limbers

7. Billets Will be left Clean & Tidy. Latrines will be filled in ½ before parade.

8. Billeting Party:- Lt HARTLEY, Sgt Heath Cpl Bates

9. Officers Kits To be in Stores by 8 am.

10. Rations Haversack Rations will be Carried
    Dinners in Billets

11. Routine Reveille 6 am
    Breakfast 6.30 am

12. Motor Transport Under Lt BARKER. To accompany lorry.
    C.Q.M.S. Bakewell, Pte Hewes, Frost.

13. General All Cooks Gear on Lorry
    Offrs Mess on Mess Cart
    Water Cart to be filled
    All vehicles to be well greased before marching off

Act. Adjt.

M. G. Company.

1   Coy Form 1.

Bty N° 2

No. 199 MACHINE GUN COMPANY.

OPERATION ORDERS. No. 5 By

CAPTAIN J. MUHLIG   Commanding 199 M.G. Coy.

At   Dated 2-3-17

	REFERENCE MAP.				
1.	This Coy In conjunction with 118th I.B. Operation orders N° 115. The Company will move into Billets at HAVER'S KIERSON.				
2.	Section No.	Gun No.	No. in Line and Position of Gun in Line	No. of Section Relieving.	No. of Gun Relieving.
	N° 4		Parade at		Transport
	N° B'n Coy H.Q. Res				Grouped
	N° 1		Move off in column of Route. H.Q. Coy at 11.5 am		as
	N° 2		Starting Point		for
	N° 3		Pass Starting Point at		days
	Billeting Party		Lt Hartley & 2 other Ranks Parade under orders of Lt Hartley		

Copy No II

OPERATION ORDERS—continued   Sheet No. 2

3. Parade: Coy Parade at 9-15 am. (Battle order) Packs on limber

4. BLANKETS. Rolled by Sections & in Stores by 8 am.

5. JERKINS. On Fighting limbers.

6. Order of March. No 1 leading. Fighting order 100ˣ between sections. Head Qrs in Rear.

7. Motor Trans. Lorry will call as usual. & loading of Stores etc will be done under supervision of Lt ELSON

8. Routine. Reveille 6.30 am
Breakfast 7. am
Dinners on arrival at LAVENTIE

9. Routine:- Fighting limbers of No 1 & 2 Sections will be packed as for Trecketts (including 1 dixie per gun)
After dinner No 1 & 2 Sections will proceed to relieve 2 Section of No 193 Coy in the line.
Limbers Returning to LAVENTIE on completion of duty.
Cooks Cart with Cooks with sufficient dixies to cook dinner & Rations will leave for LAVENTIE at 8 am
To accompany:- 2 Cooks & Cpl Bates & 3 Signallers.
(Signallers to take over from 193 Coy.)

10. Report. Report re completion of Relief & Returns of Stores Taken over (in Triplicate) will be sent to Coy Hd Qrs in LAVENTIE by Orderly as soon as Relief is completed.

11. Adv Party. Will consist of 2 Cooks, Signallers, & Trans Sgt. under command of Lt HARTLEY.

12. Lorry Party. Coy Qr Mr Sgt. Pte Pilling, Riley, Pte BOYLE, under Command of Lt ELSON

13. Special. Trench Partys will have remainder of days Rations on them. (or in Byks on limbers) as Section off. decides.

                                        W. Y. Hartley
                                                Act. Adjt.

Copy No 1. To Officers
   No 2   + Diary   199 M. G. Company.

Copy No. 1

Coy Form 1

No. 199 MACHINE GUN COMPANY.

OPERATION ORDERS. No. 6 By

Captain J. Muhlig M.C.

Commanding 199 M.G. Coy.

At Le Grand Pacaud.   Dated 4-3-17.

REFERENCE MAP.

1. The Company will relieve the 193rd M.G. Coy on the Div Front on the 5-3-17 as follows.

Section No.	Gun No.	No. in Line and Position of Gun in Line.	No. of Section Relieving.	No. of Gun Relieving.
No 1	1	No 1 Samsons Post	—	—
	2	No 2 B Line Post	—	—
	3	No 3 A.A. Post	—	—
	4	No 4 Reserve Post	—	—
No 2	5	No 5 Grants Post		
	6	No 6 O P 3		
	7	No 7 Dreadnought		
	8	No 8 Cinema House		
No 3	9, 10, 11, 12	Reserve Billets Laventie	Relieving 2	
No 4	13, 14, 15, 16	Reserve Billets Laventie	Sections of No 193 M.G. Coy	
Coy Hd Qrs		at Laventie		
Section orderlies Hd Qr Orderlies	No 2 Sect Pte Odell F. No 1 " " Odell S.J. Pte Pilling, Hawkins, Taylor.		Accompany Sections to Line. Accompany Hd Qr	

R. Huntley H/Sgt
199 M.G. Coy

Copy No 3.

No. 1(M Div) MACHINE GUN COMPANY.

OPERATION ORDERS. No. 4 By
CAPTAIN J. MUNRO M.C
Commanding M M.G. Coy.

At Laventie   Dated 10-3-17

	REFERENCE MAP. Aubers 36 SW1 Fauquissart 36 SW3				
1.	[illegible handwritten paragraph]				
2.	Section No.	Gun No.	No. in Line and Position of Gun in Line	No. of Section Relieving.	No. of Gun Relieving.
	No 3	1 Gun	at Shasses Post S.14.a.20.05	No I	1 Gun
		1 Gun	" B Line S.10.95.65		1 Gun
		1 Gun	" Lansdowne Post S.6.c.04.95		1 Gun
		1 Gun	In Reserve at [illegible] X.11.b.20.70		1 Gun
			Lansdowne Post S.6.c.04.95		
	No 4	1 Gun	at Winchester Post N.23.c.65.40	No 2	
		1 Gun	" Grants Post N.23.d.35.25		
		1 Gun	" Dreadnought Post N.23.d.55.80		
		1 Gun	" Cinema House N.24.a.12.10		
		Sec HQrs	at Winchester Post N.23.c.88.48		
	Coy HQ		[illegible] at Laventie		
	Orderlies Company Letters	No 3	Pte Hawkins		
		No 4	" Taylor		
	Transport		2 No 3 lorries will report at [illegible]		
			[illegible] at 4 p.m.		
	Guides		[illegible handwritten]		

OPERATION ORDERS—continued Sheet No. **2.**

3. [illegible] — [illegible] Sections [illegible] with them. Taking over from Sections [illegible] etc.

4. Blankets — [illegible]

5. Handing over — The following will be taken over from Relieved Sections. [illegible] Maps & Positions, [illegible] Report. [illegible]

6. Report & Returns — The following [illegible] will be handed to O C Coy by O C Sections:
Completion of Relief Report
List of Stores Handed over
[illegible]

7. Billets — [illegible]

8. Rations — [illegible] will be provided for [illegible] Sections [illegible] Rations with them.

9. Parades — Sections will [illegible]
N° 1 Section [illegible] p.m.
N° 2 [illegible] p.m.

10. [illegible] — [illegible]

11. [illegible] — [illegible]

12. [illegible] — [illegible]

[illegible] Act. Adjt.

M. G. Company.

Copy N° 1 [illegible]
2 [illegible]
3 [illegible]

1   Coy Form 1.

Copy No 3 No. 199   MACHINE GUN COMPANY.

OPERATION ORDERS.   No. 8   By
CAPT. S. MUHLIG M.C. Commanding 199 M.G. Coy.

At LAVENTIE.   Dated 16-3-17

1. REFERENCE MAP. /TRENCH. AUBERS. 36. S.W.1 & RICHEBOURG 36. S.W.3 1/10000

No 1 & 2 Sections will Relieve No 3 & 4 Sections in the Trenches on the 14th inst. On Completion of Relief No 1 & 2 Sections will return to Billets at LAVENTIE becoming Divisional Mobile Reserve.

2.

Section No.	Gun No.	No. in Line and Position of Gun in Line.	No. of Section Relieving.	No. of Gun Relieving.
No. 1	4 Guns	Right Brigade Sector	3	4 Guns
No. 2	3 Guns	Centre Brigade Sector	4	3 Guns
No. 2	1 Gun	Left Brigade Sector	4	1 Gun
Coy Hd Qrs.		Remain in LAVENTIE		
Orderlies to Accompany Section	No. 1 No. 2	Pte. Odell. S.S. " Pilling		
No 1 & 2 Sections.		When completed Relief are under the Tactical Command of the Bgde Comdr in their Sectors.		

R. Hurley Sergt
L. 199 M.G. Coy

OPERATION ORDERS—continued   Sheet No. **2**.

3. Equipment   Nos 1 & 2 Sections will take Guns & Spare Parts with them. Other
                gear will be taken over from the Sections in the line

4. Blankets   Rolled by Sections & handed into Coy Stores

5. Handing over All Trench Stores Ammn: Maps etc will be handed over to
                Relieving Sections
                No 3 Section will hand over the Coy Chronometer to No 1 Section

6. Reports etc The following Reports & Returns will be handed to O.C. Coy by
                O.C. Section relieved.
                Completion of Relief Report.
                List of Stores etc Handed over.
                " of Trench Maps & Indirect Fire forms (completed) handed over.

7. Billets etc Will be left Clean & Tidy by Outgoing Sections
                Trenches & Dugouts —"— —"— Relieved —"—

8. Rations   Tea will be provided for Relieved Sections on Return
                to Billets

9. Parade   Sections will parade for the Trenches as follows:-
                No 1 Section at 4-30 pm
                No 2   "   " 5-30 pm

10. Valises   Will be put on Limbers

11. General   Work will be carried on in accordance with progress
                Return of Relieved Sections.
                No letters or other documents likely to be of importance
                to the enemy will be taken into the Trenches
                A Box will be kept in Coy Office for any letters
                men wish to keep whilst in the line

12. Copies of O.O. Will be Returned to Coy Office on Completion of Relief.

13. Guides   As before detailed.

                                                          Act. Adjt.
                                                          M. G. Company.

Copy No 1   to O.C. No 3 Section
     2   "   "   " 4 "
     3   to Diary.

1
#gN°3/

Coy Form 1.

No. 199 MACHINE GUN COMPANY.

OPERATION ORDERS. No. 9 By

CAPTAIN S. MUNDIE M.C. Commanding 199 M.G. Coy.

At LAVENTIE   Dated 22-3-17

1.	REFERENCE MAP. TRENCH MAPS 36 S.W.1 & TRENCH MAP 36 S.W.2				
	N°3 & 4 Sections with relief N°s 1 & 2 sections in the Trenches on 23rd inst. On completion of relief N°s 1 & 2 Sections will return to Billets in LAVENTIE becoming Div. Month Reserve.				

2.	Section No.	Gun No.	No. in Line and Position of Gun in Line.	No. of Section Relieving.	No. of Gun Relieving.
	N° 3	1 Gun	Right Brigade Sector	N° 1	1 Gun
	N° 4	3 Guns	Centre Brigade Sector	2	3 Guns
	N° 4	1 Gun	Left Brigade Sector	2	1 Gun
	Coy H.Q. Coy & Transport		Remain in LAVENTIE		
	Orderlies & In-company Sections	N°3 N°4	Pte Hawkins — Odell		
	Command.		When Relief is completed Sections in Trenches come under command of Brigade Commdr. Reserve under O.C. Coy		

S. Mundie Lt. Coy.
199 M.G. Coy.

OPERATION ORDERS—continued   Sheet No. **2**.

3.
- Equipment with Guns: No. 3 & 4 Sections will take Guns & Spare Parts. Kitty bags other equipment from Sections in rear.

- 4 Blankets: Rolled by sections & handed in Stores.

- 5 Haversacks: All mail & Stores reports will be handed over to [?] section. No. 1 section will hand over all by November 6 P.B.

- 6 Reports &c: The usual Reports will be handed to OC Coy on completion of relief.

- 7 Billets: Men to keep clean & tidy. [?] & [?]

- 8 Rations: Tea will be provided for relieved sections on return to Billets.

- 9 Parades: Sections will parade for Trenches as follows:
  No. 2 section at 4.30 pm
  " 4p " " 5.15 "

- 10 Values: [illegible]

- [11?] [illegible]

- [?] Copies to O.C. [illegible] & Coy officers on [?] of Relief.

Copies No. 1
        2
        3

                                                Act. Adjt.
                                                M. G. Company.

Vol 5

SECRET.

WAR DIARY.

OF

199th Machine Gun Coy

FOR

April 1917.

Army Form C. 2118.

WAR DIARY
or
INTELLIGENCE SUMMARY

(Erase heading not required.)

PAGE 25

of 199 MACHINE GUN COMPANY

for APRIL 1917

Instructions regarding War Diaries and Intelligence Summaries are contained in F. S. Regs., Part II. and the Staff Manual respectively. Title Pages will be prepared in manuscript.

Place	Date	Hour	Summary of Events and Information	Remarks and references to Appendices
LAVENTIE	31/3/17		A mild day, rain throughout day. Snow fell during the day. Special work Anti Aircraft work. Officers & (proportion of) N.C.Os to Ferme DuBois Sector to reconnoitre lines. All returned by 3 p.m. Self to 164 Hd Qrs 164 Coy re particulars of Relief. Lt DARNELL to Field Ambulance Sick. A quiet day in Billets an uneventful 24 hrs. Sick 1 to be admitted to Field Ambulance. Strength of Company 10 Offrs 148 Other Ranks. (1 to Field Ambulance)	present (1)
LAVENTIE	1/4/17		Officers on Strength of Company: Capt. J. MUHLIG — Commdg Coy Lieut R.J. HARTLEY — 2/in Command " N.C. PORTER — Commdg No 1 Section " G. ASQUITH — " " 2 " 2/Lieut D.B. ADAM — " " 3 " " Q.C. LINDLEY — " " 4 " " R.M. THOMAS — Sub Section Offr 1 " " W.P. BARKER — " " " 2 " " R. ELSON — " " " 4 " " W.F. THORPE — Transport Offr A wet stormy day, Rain throughout day, Snow fell during the night. Company to Divine Service during forenoon. Lt HARTLEY to 164 M.G. Coy 164 Qrs found that owing to hostile shelling they had moved from SLOANE SQ to retoured. Unsuccessful 24 hours Sick Nil. Unavailable Nil. Strength of Company 10 Offrs 148. Other Ranks (1 to field Ambulance)	present
LAVENTIE	2/4/17		A cold day, Snow & Rain during day. Artillery active throughout day. Vicinity of Mule dump shelled with 4.1 mms at 3 pm. Company resumed Training, owing to inclemency of weather. Gun work indoors. Section Offrs of No C.O. to Ferme du Bois Sector to reconnoitre. Visited by O.C. 19th Lan: Fus: dump forenoon re Div Reserve Scheme. Visited by Lt Col M Gooding afternoon. Sgt ADAMSON to C.C.S. Struck off Strength accordingly. Sick. Nil Casualties. Nil Strength of Company 10 Offrs 142. Other Ranks. (2 to field ambt)	present

PAGE 26

Army Form C. 2118.

WAR DIARY
or
INTELLIGENCE SUMMARY of 199. MACHINE GUN COMPANY.

(Erase heading not required.)

for Month of APRIL 1919.

Instructions regarding War Diaries and Intelligence Summaries are contained in F.S. Regs., Part II. and the Staff Manual respectively. Title Pages will be prepared in manuscript.

Place	Date	Hour	Summary of Events and Information	Remarks and references to Appendices
LAVENTIE	3/4/14		A wild stormy morning, snow fell during forenoon, cleared up during afternoon. Inspection of Divisional Train. Company cleared up to Bathe to paid out during day. Artillery both sides active about 2p.m. Ham shells fell in vicinity of billet during afternoon, no damage. Weather 24 Hrs. Sgt Nd, Casualties Nil, Strength of Company 10 offs 147 Other Ranks. (3 Field Ambulance).	Appendix
LAVENTIE	4/4/14		A mild day, fine. Company preparing for tour in trenches. Guns etc overhauled. Self to see on my M&G Sections to LEnto FERME du Bois de Est of N. I.M. emplacements, noted proposed Corps emplacements. A quiet day. Weather 24 hrs Sgt NI, Casualties Nd, Strength of Coy 10 offs 140 O.R. (24 F.A.)	Appendix
LAVENTIE	5/4/14		A mild day. fine. Company relieved 144 M&Co make trenches FERME DU BOIS Sector. Dispositions 3 Sections in the line; 1 Section in Reserve. Coy Hd. Qrs transport situated in LE TOURET. Nos 2, 3, 4 Sections in the trenches, No 1 in Reserve at LE TOURET. Relief completed 12 noon. M.G. Coy proceeded to LES 8 MAISONS leaving Company in Divisional Reserve. Self reported to Bring H&l Qrs during evening. Guns fired 2000 Rds on hostile working parties during night. An uneventful 24 hours. Sect Nl, Casualties Nl. Strength of Company 10 offs 140 Other Ranks (2 Field amb)	Appendix
LE TOURET	6/4/14		A cold day, rain during forenoon. Reserve Section busy improving Billets. An even built. About 5pm about 123 shells 4.4mm fell into Billet area. No damage done. Sections in line quiet. Self Reconnoitred Right Section area, returned at 5pm thence to Bring to report. Guns in line fired 1200 Rds at hostile working parties. Sect R2, L/c Norman & CQMS Br. SMITH to 34 Field Amb, Pt SMITH to Field Amb. Pt BARNELL to CQM Sgt BARNELL to 8th hours Casualties Nd, Strength of Coy 100ff=169 O.R. (4 Field amb)	Appendix
LE TOURET	7/4/14		A mild day. fine. Artillery very active on both sides. Aerial activity throughout day. Self to Lavin in reconnaissance of Centre Section & Right Section. Guns in line quiet. Guns in line fired 4800 Rds during the night on to hostile back areas. Received Re. inforcement of 1 Pte. (Sommer) A quiet + uneventful 24 hours. Strength Sect Nil, Casualties Nil, Strength of Company 10offs 140 other Ranks. (4 Field Ambulance)	Appendix
LE TOURET	8/4/14		A hot, mild day, clear + bright. Self to Left Section at PONT LOGY. Reconnaissance of enemy lines at H.M. McInnes dd Res. Section M.E. O red Ribbed scheme. Stroll artillery action on half areas in vicinity of billets abolish by 4.4mm during forenoon, no damage done, Pt Whitehouse to Base, L/C Norman + Pt Crispin to C.C. Station. Struck off Strength, CQMS BARNELL to duty from Field Amb, Sgt Nd Casualties Nd, been in line fires 8700 Rds during night. An uneventful 24 hours, Strength of Company 10 offs 149 O.R. (2 Field amb)	Appendix

2449 Wt. W14957/M90 750,000 1/16 J.B.C. & A. Forms/C.2118/12.

PAGE. 2 M.

WAR DIARY of No. 199 MACHINE GUN COMPANY
INTELLIGENCE SUMMARY
Month of APRIL 1917

Army Form C. 2118.

Place	Date	Hour	Summary of Events and Information	Remarks and references to Appendices
LE TOURET	9/4/16		A stormy morning. Artillery active throughout day. No 1 Section relieved No 2 Section in the Right Section area. Relief completed by 10am. No 2 Section to Reserve Billets. A quiet day in area of Billets. Section defence scheme completed & issued to Sections in Sinks. Buses on limbers from Bovis Rds during the night on Battle Back areas. An uneventful 24 hours. Sick Nil. 16 casualties Nil. Strength of Company 10 Off: 164 Other Ranks. (1 Field Ambulance)	Answer [signature]
LE TOURET	10/4/17		A wild day. Stormy, high wind blowing. Snow at intervals throughout day. G.O.C. division inspected transport during the afternoon. Thermometer dropped near Fosse during the early hours of the morning a mule strayed from lines & though followed for some distance is still missing. During the night 1+8 O.R. carried the enemy's trenches. Reparatory cutting & along Guards Trench up to 11-30 p.m. Otherwise a quiet night. Buses fired 6,900 Rds during night on Battle Back areas. Sick Nil. Casualties Nil. Strength of Coy 10 Off 164 O.R. (1 F.A.)	Answer [signature]
LE TOURET	11/4/17		An inclement day, cold & snow throughout day & night. Self visited all Sections in the line. Found all correct & well on rounds of No 3 Section. A quiet uneventful 24 hours. Double Artillery sentries. 2 were posted a dusk. Other Reinforcement on Battle Back areas. 1 Mule still missing. Pte Whiston rejoined Coy from adv. A.T. Depot as a Driver. Other Ranks Strength 16 for No 3 depot. No 1 P.R. from Base depot. Cpl Bunter & Pass from Nos Strength & Strength accordingly. Sick Nil. Casualties Nil. Strength of Company 10 Off/17 141 Other Ranks (4 F.A.N.S.)	Answer [signature]
TRENCHES Fme du Bois	12/4/17		A cold day, showers of rain throughout day. Strong wind blowing. Self visited Sections in line. Found all correct & Yates O.R. Hd Qrs during evening. Warmly reconnoitred line. Stormy afternoon. A quiet 24 hours Active artillery during night. Sick Nil Casualties Nil. Strength of Coy 10 Off/17 141 Other Ranks.	Answer [signature]
TRENCHES Fme du Bois	13/4/17		A fine day, quite mild. During forenoon No 2 Section relieved No 3 Section in Centre Section. Relief completed without incident at 11.30 p.m. No 3 Section to Reserve Billets at Le Touret. Improvement carried out in Trenches during afternoon. Right Artillery bombarded S.E. etc. Very little retaliation. Buses fired 8900 Rds during the night on Battle Back areas. An uneventful 24 hours Sick Nil. Casualties Nil. Strength of Company 10 Off/17 141 Other Ranks. (4 A H.D)	Answer [signature]
TRENCHES Fme du Bois	14/4/17		A fine day mild. Strong Wind blowing. No 1 Gun Team Reserve Section Hit Gun & Team to Baths during forenoon. Worked on Trenches immediately afternoon. Sick Nil. Casualties Nil. Buses fired 4900 Rds during night. Strength of Coy 10 Off 141 O.R.	Answer [signature]

WAR DIARY / INTELLIGENCE SUMMARY

Page 28 — No. 199 Machine Gun Company — 1st April 1914 [1914]

Army Form C. 2118.

Place	Date	Hour	Summary of Events and Information	Remarks and references to Appendices
TRENCHES Fme du Bois Sect.	15/4/14		A wet day. Rain throughout day. Reserve section to Divine services during forenoon. Pt Tyrell accidentally wounded thumb during shelling exe. A quiet day. Sey to Bty Hd Qrs. Infantry reinforcements carried but on transport limes during day. Arg Sen 1/14 9 Army Vickers Bursts during evening. A quiet & uneventful 24 hours. Sick Nil, Casualties Nil. Strength of Coy 10 Offr 141 other Ranks. Pris 9000 Rds during night.	Accept
TRENCHES Fme du Bois Sect.	16/4/14		A fine day, bright cold. Aerial activity throughout day. Reserve section Farms during forenoon. Sey to Divine Service all sections. Anti Aircraft Batt near billets action during forenoon Relics during evening might. M.G. fire 2000 Rds during night, otherwise an uneventful 24 hours. Sick Nil. Casualties Nil Strength of Company 10 Offr 141 other Ranks.	Accept
TRENCHES Fme du Bois Sect.	17/4/14		A stormy day, rain during forenoon, cleared up during afternoon. High wind throughout day. No 3 Section relieved Nº 4 section in time Right section during morning. Relief completed correctly 11 am. Nº 4 Section to Reserve Billets. A bad night run of rained whole night. Guns on line fired 9000 Rds during night in both base area. An uneventful 24 hours. Sick Nil Casualties Nil. Strength of Coy 10 Offr 141 other Ranks.	Accept
TRENCHES Fme du Bois Sect.	18/4/14		A cold day. Rain & wind throughout day. Reserve section to Baths. Sey to Les Huit Maisons to my Car relief by Elsham. Reconful Reinforcements from Base, consisting of 1 officer & 4 Pte. Officer 2/Lt T.B. Francis posted to M.G. section as sub-section offr 1 Pte to No 1 Section. 3 Ptes to No 2 Section. Physical standards of Reinforcements up to manual. Quite good. Sick Pt Wood to 05 F.A. from Trenches. A quiet & uneventful 24 hours. Guns in base fired 4500 Rds on hostile Roads area during night. Sick Offr Casualties Nil. Strength of Coy 10 Offr 145 OR (1Fr)	Accept
TRENCHES Fme du Bois Sect.	19/4/14		Another wet day. Showers of rain throughout day. Sey visited Sections in time during forenoon. Reconful Reinforcements from Base, consisting of bullets on relief. Issues Coy Operation orders & Map to Harney to 11/Coy Hd Qrs at Les Huit Maisons ne distribution of bullets with clean bill of health. A quiet uneventful 24 hours on Bivv's Veterinary inspection of all animals; persons in hustle back areas during night. Sick Nil Casualties Nil. Strength Coy 11 Offr 145 OR (1Fr) Guns fired 4500 Rds on hostile Back areas during night.	Accept
TRENCHES Fme du Bois Sect.	20/4/14		A fine day, left round dmb with Corps M.G.O. visited all new Corps positions found them all in state of construction. The day was spent on the hut by 11/# MLe Coy Reliefs commenced at 8.30 am d was completed by 11 am. Company on Reliefs proceeded to Les Huits Maisons becoming on Reserve Coy; heavy bullets in huts. Quite good. Sick & Quiet uneventful 24 hrs. Sick Nil, Casualties Nil. Strength of Coy 11 Offr 145 OR (1Fr W)	Accept

WAR DIARY

of No 199 MACHINE GUN COY

for APRIL 1917

PAGE 29.

Army Form C. 2118.

Place	Date	Hour	Summary of Events and Information	Remarks and references to Appendices
LES HUITS MAISONS.	21/4/17		A fine day. Company engaged cleaning up & Kit Inspection after the tour in the line. Coy visited Off commdg 1st Rsrve during afternoon. Also reconnoitred emergent roads & areas in divisional front. Genuine activit during day. Otherwise a quiet & uneventful 24 hours. ↑ & W flying K & dis Amb. sect. Casualties Nil. Strength of Coy 11 Offrs 146 O.R. (24 Q.R.) The tour in the trenches was the 19th from in the line as a company, it is doubtful we rank much good. Enemy apparently was in a state of nervousness, the enemy especially so knowledged machine gun fire during the night doubtful we might be effective enough to the enemy. On actual (occasion front of the fire's emergency effort was given by hostile bursts of fire, shrapnel, over the vicinity of the guns firing. On several occasions the men were under a more or less heavy hostile shell fire, the absence of casualties gave them great confidence in themselves and improves their morale to a great extent. On the whole a decidedly experience for all ranks.	Vincent
LES HUITS MAISONS.	22/4/17		A fine day, bright but rather cold. Company to Divine Service at VIEUX CHAPELLE during afternoon. Recruits 9th Reinforcement from Base. 1 Cpl 10 LCpls 16th Ford Bn 1st N.Z.O. wounded. Patrols 1st N°2 sections. Bombardment on Right of our area during night. A quiet uneventful 24 hrs. All offrs recommended. War Diary. Cas Nil. Casualties Nil. Strength of Coy 11 offrs 146 O.R.G.Y.O.	Vincent
LES HUITS MAISONS.	23/4/17		A fine day, Company to Baths. Instruments carried out on Bullets of Ross Emes during day; including the testing of our sneck & washelock. Visited by Q.S.O.! DHI during afternoon. Patrols returned; all officers arrived. Reconnaissance of our area continued. A quiet uneventful 24 hours. Sick Nil. Casualties Nil. Strength of Coy 11 offrs 146 O.R (2 Z.O).	Vincent
LES HUITS MAISONS.	24/4/17		A fine day, bright, but cold wind. Reconnaissance of our area by offrs completed. Coy during forenoon. Lew Drill & Lecture during afternoon. Genl activit during day. Recruits 10th Reinft duri Base, 11 O.R. (includ. the Church returned) (Patrols 2 to No 1 & 2 to N°3 Section. Sick Nil. Casualties Nil. A quiet uneventful 24 hours. Strength of Coy 11 offrs 180 other Ranks (2 field Ambulance).	Vincent
LES HUITS MAISONS.	25/4/17		A fine day, rather cold. Medical Inspection of Company during day. Clean bill of health. Veterinary inspection of animals during day. Tactical scheme by all officers during evening. Company at Gun or or deroy day. Gas drill during afternoon. Sick 1. Pt Cummins to 2 A Casualties Nil. Strength of Coy 11 Offrs 180 O.R. (2 fld). A quiet uneventful 24 hours.	Vincent

WAR DIARY

INTELLIGENCE SUMMARY

Army Form C. 2118.

of No. 199. MACHINE GUN COMPANY.

for APRIL 1917.

PAGE 30

Place	Date	Hour	Summary of Events and Information	Remarks and references to Appendices
LES HUITS MAISONS.	26/4/17		A fine day, rather cold, bright. Genl. DeKitz during day. 2nd Lt. HARNEY & No. 8 by Hd. Qrs. at LE DRUMEZ to look over billets & huts. All officers & NCOs to various sectors of Line Neuve Chapelle Sector for reconnaissance. Self visited O.C. 141st Inf. Bde. in LAVENTIE in conjunction with Bde. Reco'nce Scheme. Company route march during forenoon. Sick one to C.Y.EUREN to Field Amb. Pnr. BOYS burst one dummy percussion during early morning. One of the test mules was kicked in the eye & rather badly hurt. A quiet night. Casualties. Nil Strength of Company 11 Offrs. 180 O.R. (H&A)	Absent (signed)
LES HUITS MAISONS.	27/4/17		A fine day, rather cold. Self to 148 Coy. Hd. Qrs. re Relief. Company engaged on a tactical schemes during afternoon. Getting ready for the relief. Pte. Smith & Pte. Panego to 5 F.A. Sick. Pte. Flood to C.C.S. Struck off strength. A quiet & uneventful 24 hours. Casualties. Sick R 2 Casualties. Nil. Strength of Company 11 Offrs. 149 Other Ranks 5. Field Ambulance	Absent (signed)
TRENCHES NEUVE CHAPELLE SECTOR	28/4/17		A fine day. Company relieved the 148 M.G. Coy. in the trenches Neuve Chapelle Sector. Disposition 3 Sections (12 Guns) in the Line, 1 Section in Reserve. Company Hd. Qr. at 8 am completed with relief. At 12-30 p.m. 148 M.G. Coy. the previous occupants proceeded to LES HUITS MAISONS became Bde. Res. Self reported to Brig. Hd. Qrs. during evening. A quiet uneventful 24 hours. Gnr. frey Boro Pte. Dunning the night. Sick Nil. Casualties. Nil. Strength of Company 11 Offrs. 149 Other Ranks (5 Field Amb.)	Absent (signed)
TRENCHES NEUVE CHAPELLE SECTOR	29/4/17		A fine day, warm & bright. O.C. Coy visited Right Section in line during forenoon. Decided on position for machine gun to worry hostile communication trenches. Hostile artillery active against Rouge Croix Cross Road during day. O.C. Coy & Party to Company HQ during evening. re South on various matters that came up during afternoon. Mr. Porter proceeded to 148 G.B. School then previous work. Nil Section with 2 Guns under Mr. Porter proceeded to 148 G.B. School then part in a School tactical scheme. A good practice which was of value to the personnel. Mr. Whatley to C.C.S. Struck off strength accordingly. Sick Nil. Casualties. Nil. Strength of Company 11 Offrs. 148 other Ranks (4 sick Ambulance) – Lieu Price Corp R Wells joining	Absent (signed)

30.4.14

(signed) Captain
Commanding 199 Machine Gun Coy.

Copy No 2

Coy Form 1

No. 199   **MACHINE GUN COMPANY.**

OPERATION ORDERS.   No. 11   By

CAPTAIN. S. MUHLIG M.C.   Commanding 199 M.G. Coy.

At LAVENTIE.   Dated 4-4-17.

REFERENCE MAP. TRENCH RICHEBOURG 36 S.W.3 1/10000

1. In accordance with H.Q. 184 O.O. No 103 The Company will relieve the 144th Bde M.G. Coy in the line on the 5-4-17. Relief to be completed by 5 p.m.

2.

Section No.	Gun No	No. in Line and Position of Gun in Line.	No. of Section Relieving.	No. of Gun Relieving.
No. 2 Orderly Pte HAWKINS	1 Gun 1 Gun 1 Gun 1 Gun S.H.Q	S15 c.8.3. S15 a.9.1 S15 b.5.4 S9 d.2.8 Anti Aircraft S9 d.2.8.	No. I 144. Coy Right Sect.	1 Gun 1 Gun 1 Gun 1 Gun
No. 3 Orderly Pte Odell. F	1 Gun 1 Gun 1 Gun 1 Gun S.H.Q	S9 d.9.3. S10 c.1.6 S10 c.3.8 S10 d.1.8 S9 d.2.8	No. 2 144 Centre Sect.	1 Gun 1 Gun 1 Gun 1 Gun
No. 4 Orderly Pte Odell. S.J.	1 Gun 1 Gun 1 Gun 1 Gun S H Q	S4 d.2.2 S5 c. 9.0 Kings Cross S5 c.9.0 Ack Aircraft S4 c.9 M34 c.1 Post Loop	No. 3 144 Left Sect.	
No. I	4 Guns	In Reserve at X 10 c. 3.4.	No. 4 144 Res Sect	4 Guns
Coy H. Qrs.	Officers & Signals	X 10 c. 3.4. W. of Emerson Rd	C.H.Q 144 Coy	
TRANSPORT	Mules & Wagon Lines	X 10 c. 3.4 W. of Emerson Rd.	Trans. 144 Coy.	

S. Muhlig Capt
199 M.G. Coy.

OPERATION ORDERS—continued   Sheet No. 2.

3. RATIONS. Rations for current day will be taken into lines with rations (No 1 section except)
Rations for coming day will arrive at WINDY CORNER about 8.30 p.m.
Ration Parties will be arranged for that stores.

4. BLANKETS. Rolled by sections & to stores by 6.45 am

5. Reveille. Reveille 5 am   Breakfast 6 am

6. PACKS. Will be put on fighting limbers

7. BROWN STORES. All pack stores Revolvers Ammn Belt Boxes etc will be taken over & lists in duplicate rendered to O.C. Coy

8. GUIDES. Guides for Gun Teams will be at Section Head Qrs of 14/Coy Sections

9. PARADE. No 2 Section Parades at 8 am   Arrive WINDY CORNER at 9 am
   " 3 "   "   " 8.30 "   "   "   "   9.30 am
   " 4 "   "   " 9 "   "   "   "   10 am
   " 1 "   Field Parade at 9.15 am

10. TRANSPORT. 1 fighting limber per section will proceed to WINDY CORNER with Sections
Returning to Coy HdQrs X10c5.4 on completion of duty.
S.A.A. limber will proceed with first load & future S.A.A. loads
to new Hd Qrs from WINDY CORNER coming on with the Sect.

1 limber packed with Belt Boxes will proceed to Hd Qrs of Coy
at X.24 A.49 at 9 A.M. under charge of Sgt Coates, on handing Boxes
over, to proceed to YPRES CHATEAU + draw full kits before
proceeding to X10c5.4 (new Hd Qrs)

Remainder of Transport will under orders of Lt HARVEY
march to new Hd Qrs at 9.30 a.m.

11. BILLETS. Billets & Transport will be inspected at 8.45 am.
Latrines etc will be wiped & clean.

12. MOTOR BUSES. Arrive at 8.30   To be loaded by 9 am
No 1 Section for loading

13. ADVANCE PARTY. To leave HdQrs by 8 am

14. COMMUNICATION. O.C. & Sgt of Section + Pte Pearce & Pearce will travel to WINDY
CORNER with No 2 & + return partway ? as ??
will wait for reports from Section lorries (2 & 3. (R. Pce.)
+ (No 4. Pte Taylor.) On receiving reports they will proceed to
New Hd Qrs.

R.V. Harvey Lt Act. Adjt.
199   M. G. Company.

Copy No 1 Officer
   " 2 14/Coy
   " 3 Diary

199. MACHINE GUN COMPANY.

Programme of Reliefs in the Trenches from 5th to 20th April 1917.

APRIL.

Section	5th	6th	7th	8th	9th	10th	11th	12th	13th	14th	15th	16th	17th	18th	19th	20th	Remarks
No 1	▓	▓	▓	▓	Relvd. by 2 on night	L	L	L	L	L	L	L	L	L	L	Relvd by 1st Coy	Shaded Portion denotes Time in Rest Billets
No 2	L	L	L	L	▓	▓	▓	▓	Relvd by 3 on night	L	L	L	L	L	L	Relvd by 1st Coy	—
No 3	L	L	L	L	L	L	L	L	▓	▓	▓	▓	Relvd by 4 on Left	L	L	Relvd by 1st Coy	Battn while Resting
No 4	L	L	L	L	L	L	L	L	L	L	L	L	▓	▓	▓	▓	

L - L - L

[signature]
Commanding 199 M.G. Coy

M194/

From - Officer Commdg
    199 Machine Gun Coy

To HdQrs 9th Division
            A Branch

                            31-5-17

Herewith War Diary of above named
Company for Month of May 1917.

                    [signature] Capt
                Commdg 199 MG Coy

WAR DIARY or INTELLIGENCE SUMMARY

Army Form C. 2118.

No. 199 MACHINE GUN COMPANY.

for MAY 1914

Place	Date	Hour	Summary of Events and Information	Remarks and references to Appendices
TRENCHES NEUVE CHAPELLE SECTOR	30/4/18		A fine day. Recent section to No. 8 Pony School. Re-tactical exercise with Infantry. Good practice for them. O.C. Coy to Trenches. Found nearly all belts required overhauling & a lot of repairs & improvements to positions necessary. Returned during afternoon. Repairs carried out in billets. Pt. Garland to E.C.S. Strucke off strength accordingly. Pt. Toseland to D Army Cookery School at Berthonv for Cookery course. Visited by No. 8 Pony Transport Off. during forenoon. A great improvement in Horses in Billets & Trenches. Guns fired 6,500 Res during the night on hostile back Areas. Sick out. 1st Tomm.. Particulars sent to details. Casualties Nil Strength of Company. 11 Off 144 other Ranks (2 Field Amb)	Anapet
TRENCHES NEUVE CHAPELLE SECTOR	1/5/18		Roll of Officers on Strength of Company 1st May 1914 Capt. J. MUHLIG — Commanding Lieut. R.J. HARTLEY — 2/in Command " E.W. PORTER — Comm'g A Section " G. ASQUITH — " B " 2/Lt D.B. ADAM — " C " " A.C. KINGSLEY — " D " 2/Lt R.M. THOMAS — Sub Sect Off. A " W.P. BARKER — " " B " R. ELSON — " " C " T.B. FRANCIS — " " D " W.F. THORPE — Transport Off. A fine day, warm & bright. O.C. Coy to Trenches. Reconnoitred Centre Section in the Line Recent Section to Battn. Received 11th Reinforcement from Base, 1 Renewed, posted to No.2 Section. Confusion of Portuguese by From Armentières on LA BASSE ROAD on account of Rouge Croix being shelled during the day for instructions, proceeding to the Trenches. Pony Ono during the night ear hire fired 6,500 Rds during the night on hostile back area. Ruby out M.S. ambo. During the previous month the discipline of the company produced little to amp, retaliation by the enemy has been very good, no serious casts have been dealt with. The moral of the personnel is good. Great compliment on Slow M Town'd been found, due chiefly to having to subjected to several heavy hostile bombardments without any Casualties. Staff No. Casualties Nil. Strength of Company 11 Off. 148 O.R. (2 F. amb Amb)	Anapet

Army Form C.2118.

PAGE 32.

WAR DIARY of No 199. MACHINE GUN COMPANY.

INTELLIGENCE SUMMARY for MAY. 1914.

(Erase heading not required.)

Place	Date	Hour	Summary of Events and Information	Remarks and references to Appendices
TRENCHES. NEUVE CHAPELLE SECTOR	2/5/14		A fine day. Warm & bright. Aerial activity throughout day. No 1 Section relieved No 2 Section in the Centre section of Pong Front during the forenoon. Relief completed without incident at 11 am. O.C. Coy to HQ 116 M.G. Coy during forenoon re preparations for a raid being carried out by the 1st 4th Regt. & 2 British troops. During the afternoon, considerable enemy activity. Porte du Hem was heavily shelled on trestle back areas during the night. No retaliation. Sick Nil. Casualties Nil. A quiet uneventful 24 hours in area. Strength of Company 11 Offrs 148 Other Ranks. (2 Field Ambs)	Annexed
TRENCHES. NEUVE CHAPELLE SECTOR	3/5/14		A fine day, warm & bright. O.C. Coy reconnoitred Left section in trenches, suggests a lot of improvements to positions that could be carried out. Evans' Post, position was shelled during forenoon & the parapet badly knocked about. Repairs carried out. Artillery Lot active Throughout day. Enemy fired 4503 Rds during night – no retaliation. O.C. Coy visited Brigade Hd Qrs during night. D of sundry action 24 hours. 4000 th artillery & trench mortars shelled most of M.G. positions during day & night. (Sick Nil. (Cpl Jones to Field Ambs) Casualties Nil. Strength of Coy 11 Offrs 148 Other Ranks (3 Field Ambulances)	Annexed
TRENCHES. NEUVE CHAPELLE SECTOR	4/5/14		A fine day, warm & bright. Aerial activity throughout day. A good deal of night flying. Seems to be taking place lately but details of aeroplanes do not known to Coy. O.C. Coy to Annex. Red reconnaissance of Left & Centre sections during forenoon. Right section head Qrs at EBENEZER FARM. Heavily shelled during the afternoon. O.C. arranged targets etc. in co-operation with 116 Pony Regd. Pt Smith to C.C.S. Shrivell Pte Strong acordingly. A good Several machine guns Expect for Pte Smith. Except for reserves of tanks down in Line fired 6,500 Rds during the night. 1 to 4 tanks taken. No retaliation. Except for reserves of tanks Shelling, an uneventful 24 hrs. Sick Nil. Casualties Nil. Strength of Coy 11 Offrs 144 other Rks (2 Field Amb)	Annexed
TRENCHES. NEUVE CHAPELLE SECTOR	5/5/14		A fine day. Aerial activity throughout day. O.C. Coy reconnoitred Right section in the house during forenoon. to Pomepelines Conferred with my enemy section in event of hostile voluntary retirement discussed. Enemy fired 6,250 Rds during night no retaliation. A quiet uneventful 24 hours Sick Nil. Casualties Nil. Strength of Coy 11 Offrs 144 other Rks (2 Field Ambs)	Annexed
TRENCHES. NEUVE CHAPELLE SECTOR	6/5/14		A fine day. Cold wind during day. Roads very dusty. O.C. Coy to Hd Qrs 116 Coy during forenoon. & to Pony Hd Qrs & down afternoon. Made arrangements for co-operation re bombardment of Bois du BIEZ with gas shells. O.C. Coy to know No.2 Section returned at M.M. made all arrangement with O.C. left section re M.G. co-operation re operation against Bois du Biez. during night returned No 3 Section – Repp Section of time during forenoon. Relief completed without incident at 11 am. Enemy fired 9,500 Rds during the night & by 4 Mags. 4,000 in co-operation. A quiet 24 hours. Cpl Jones from 3d Field Ambulance Sick Nil, Casualties Nil. Strength of Company 11 Offrs 144 Other Ranks (1 Field Ambulance).	Annexed

2449 Wt.W14957/M90 750,000 1/16 J.B.C. & A. Forms/C.2118/12.

PAGE 33

WAR DIARY / INTELLIGENCE SUMMARY

Army Form C. 2118.

of No 199 MACHINE GUN COMPANY

for MAY 1914

Place	Date	Hour	Summary of Events and Information	Remarks and references to Appendices
TRENCHES NEUVE CHAPELLE SECTOR	4/5/17		A fine day. O.C. busy in Office during forenoon, during afternoon proceeded to the three various M.G. sections. 3 N.C.O.'s to the Divisional M.G. School for training as M.G. Gas NCO. O.C. to number during evening to make arrangements for a barrage for following raids. During the night 2 raids were carried out against the hostile trenches with the object of securing an identification & inflicting casualties. Our raid was by infantry from 1/4th & 1/8th By & 1/4th by 1/4/8th Beng Rifles assisted by putting a barrage of bullets on hostile back areas. Raid was successful. Enemy's little retaliation was given. Only the enemy all was quiet by 11pm. During the night the Civic Alarm was sounded from the trenches but except for few gas shells on night of sector no other gas was felt. At 3 a.m a violent barrage of H.E. & shrapnel was put on the hostile positions on the B301 the B32. This was in connection with an operation on which the M.G.'s gave no assistance. There was no projectiles into the wood. Owing to the ambush burnable went up the gun was not sent out but each gun fired 500 rounds. L.C. Osborne (the company Clerk) was admitted to field Ambulance. P. Tayler appointed N.G. Clerk. 4 buses & lorries 21 hrs hrs. Sick (not) Nil. Strength 12 off 11 offrs 143 other ranks. Guns fired 10000 Rds during the 24 hours.	(signed)
TRENCHES NEUVE CHAPELLE SECTOR	8/5/17		Weather cold warm & bright. Relieved throughout day. Round's section to Brigade school for a Tactical exercise. O.C. out to the all sections in line, found all correct. Hy Pk Pa. to Tremblai to return to Dicourt. During night the cancelled gas attack was laid on. About 11pm it became much less host. At about 12m a & 12 midnight to 1st infantry to take Ambutane ditch independent trial out against Ferme du Bois ridge all quiet by 12 m W St. Andre Lambert & Buke rues during the night. Andreant & matinal & dulce was over. Guns fired 9000 Rds. Guns 3 full Limbers. Sect out Troville M.G. Strength of Company 11 officers 144 other Ranks.	(signed)
TRENCHES NEUVE CHAPELLE SECTOR	9/5/17		A fine day, quite warm & bright. Relief actively throughout day. (Osborne section to take up positions at Pont du Hem during forenoon). A quiet day, during night shots Dumberment houses out on Brigade front. Lost 20 minutes missing a guns messengers & her cans fell out just 350 Ods his night on hostile areas. Team: (3 N.G. L. Cert). Maxim from the enemy. Sick Nil casualties Nil. Strength of Company 11 offrs 144 other Ranks.	(signed)
TRENCHES NEUVE CHAPELLE SECTOR	10/5/17		A fine day, warm & bright. Quiet all day throughout day. No 3 section relieves O. section in Right sector by 1pm. Very comfortable without incident until 12 to Pecond in a Reciprocal from Bow her story. 1 Gunnel petits' to E.A.O.G. also withdrawn on relief & Centre section during day. Sect Nil casualties Nil. Strength of by 11 offrs 145 other rks (5th Bn). A quiet uneventful 24 hours. Guns fired 5,200 Rds out on hostile back areas during night.	(signed)

PAGE DK.

WAR DIARY of **No. 199 MACHINE GUN COMPANY**

INTELLIGENCE SUMMARY for **MAY 1914.**

Army Form C. 2118.

Instructions regarding War Diaries and Intelligence Summaries are contained in F. S. Regs., Part II. and the Staff Manual respectively. Title Pages will be prepared in manuscript.

(Erase heading not required.)

Place	Date	Hour	Summary of Events and Information	Remarks and references to Appendices
TRENCHES. NEUVE CHAPELLE SECTOR	11/5/14		A fine day, warm & bright. O C Coy reported to Brig Hd Qrs at 10 a.m. & orders to take over Anti Aircraft defences of Army dumps at Gd Servant & Rubecq. also about at MERVILLE. Reconnoitred area in company with G.S.O.2. 61st Divn & Lt LINDLEY. Arranged Reliefs etc at Rubecq. At 2 p.m. N°4 Section Lt LEDRUMEZ for Rubecq, took over defence, becoming detached from the Company for Tactical purposes. They were replaced — recruits at LEDRUMEZ by a section from 148 M.G. Coy under command of Lt DUTHOIR. KHARTEY to VIEUX CHAPELLE during afternoon to reconnoitre Buttes area. O C Coy attended a Conference of Commd Offrs during the evening. Noted that the Corps selected time of M.G. positions were complete & ready for use. During the evening a Portuguese Battn took over the Right Section of the 146 Brig, all ranks notified of Artillery tactics adopted throughout day on both sides M. G's. & time fires 5,000 Rds per hostile dark areas during the night. Suk Hd. Casualties Nil. Strength of Company 11 Offrs 148 other Ranks. (3 Field Ambulances)	[signature]
TRENCHES. NEUVE CHAPELLE SECTOR	12/5/14		A fine day, warm & bright. Great aerial activity on both sides during day. O C Coy to 148 Bay Hd Qrs at VIEUX CHAPELLE during forenoon, to arrange relief in line. On this occasion, having asked what (whenever) possible, make up plate to take place in all the Coys sub sections etc, as the firing over of Belt boxes etc leads in the end to much recommendation as to state of ammunition etc. During the afternoon a sub section of No. 1 Section at SURPRISE POST was relieved by a sub section of 148 M.G. Coy from VIEUX CHAPELLE. This sub section returned to Coy Hd Qrs at LEDRUMET & left for MERVILLE in the afternoon to relieve a sub section of 148 Coy engaged in Anti Aircraft defence. They were under command of 2 Lt THOMAS. Near the hostile trenches opposite our front to the 144th Bd Divn from Vimy, there do not seem so enterprising as the 61 Bd Divn whom plain shelly had taken. During the afternoon there was a desultory shelling of GIVENCHY Post by hostile guns, in course of which one other Rank (Pte TAYLOR) was wounded. A quiet night. Rumors fired 5000 Rds on hostile trench beacons during night. Paying particular attention to the Sector SUNKEN ROAD S. E. had AUBERS to BAS POMMEREAU, as it is reputed that a Left (H/W) loop is being driven there. SUK Hd. Casualties 1.O.R. wounded. Strength of Coy 11 Offrs 147 other Ranks. (3 Field Ambulances)	[signature]
TRENCHES. NEUVE CHAPELLE SECTOR	13/5/14		A fine day, showers of rain during the afternoon. The Company was relieved in the line by the 148 M.S. Coy. Relief commenced at 9 a.m completed by 11.30 a.m. Company in relay to Dv Reserve Coy, billets at VIEUX CHAPELLE. During the afternoon sub section of No. 1 Section proceeded to MERVILLE for Anti Aircraft duties, when complete the section to report to Mudros Command Lt PORTER. This section recommenced under the Tactical Command of O C Coy & has orders to rejoin Coy on what of a hostile attack. Billets in VIEUX CHAPELLE had O C Coy to DN Hd Qrs during some are changes, letters preparation etc. to do so grades. Sect Dun (Pte ROBERTS & Et A) Casualties Nil. Strength of Coy 11 Offrs 147 OR (not a ...	[signature]

2449 Wt. W14957/M90 750,000 1/16 J.B.C. & A. Forms/C.2118/12.

PAGE 25.

Army Form C. 2118.

WAR DIARY or INTELLIGENCE SUMMARY

199 MACHINE Gun COMPANY

for MAY 1914

Instructions regarding War Diaries and Intelligence Summaries are contained in F. S. Regs., Part II. and the Staff Manual respectively. Title Pages will be prepared in manuscript.

(Erase heading not required.)

Place	Date	Hour	Summary of Events and Information	Remarks and references to Appendices
Reserve Billets VIEUX CHAPELLE	14/5/14		A fine day. Showers of rain throughout day. O C Coy to MERVILLE to see N° 1 Section. Found all correct. 4 HARTLEY to ZELOBES during afternoon to reconnoitre new billets, found quite adequate. Billets to 3 times. A quiet uneventful 24 hours. (Reserve Section spent day cleaning up. Sick Nil Casualties Nil. Strength of Coy 11 offs 144 O.R. (4 + a)	Appx [sig]
Reserve Billets VIEUX CHAPELLE	15/5/14		A fine day, warm & bright. During the afternoon Coy moves to new billets at ZELOBES. Move completed within the day. O C Coy to LAVENTIE to see C.O of Div Reserve. Move complete except for signals which arrive at Vielle Chapelle for the present. A quiet uneventful 24 hours. Sanitary arrangements carried out in new billets. Sick Nil Casualties Nil. Strength of Coy 11 offs 144 other Ranks. (3 Field Amb)	Appx [sig]
Reserve Billets ZELOBES	16/5/14		A change in the weather, cold & dull, rain during afternoon & evening. O.C. Coy to HINGES to see Corps M.G. officer. HARTLEY & HINGES for Coach, Reed Company Rest during afternoon. Reserve sections to Baths during forenoon. H HINDLEY to Hd Qrs from ROSTCQ returning evening reports all satisfactory. Lilt Edson & 5 other O.R.s to R Cutts A.A at Pont for Coy gas instruction. An A.A wire. A quiet uneventful 24 hours. Sick Nil Casualties Nil. Strength of Company 11 offrs 144 other Ranks. 3 Field Ambulance	Appx [sig]
Reserve Billets ZELOBES	17/5/14		A wet day, cold & dull. Reserve Sections & Gun numbers M Kits & cleaning up. 4 HARTLEY/ADAM - went reconnoitre low area during forenoon. Improvement of Billets carried out evident, it was soon done over the billets had been occupied or they had got into a muddy state, this applies specially to the horse lines (Lt Archer returned from field Ambulance. A quiet uneventful 24 hours. Sick Nil. Strength of Coy 11 offrs 149 O.R. (2 + a)	Appx [sig]
Reserve Billets ZELOBES	18/5/14		A fine day, bright & warm, aerial activity during day. Sections at Gun Drill during forenoon. Gun Drill during afternoon. A quiet uneventful 24 hours. One Coy & Section offrs reconnoitre New front during evening. Sick Nil. Casualties Nil. Strength of Company 11 offs 140 O.R. (2 + a)	Appx [sig]
Reserve Billets ZELOBES	19/5/14		A fine day, bright & warm. Aerial activity during day. O C Coy & Lt Hartley to Hd Qrs 145 M Gun Coy at LAVENTIE to arrange details of relief. O E Coy visited Commdt Div Reserve. Reserve Section Route March during forenoon, all section offrs to MERVILLE to reconnoitre Aerial defence. A quiet uneventful 24 hours. Sick 2. Pte Moxwell & Millett. Both to 54 C.C.S. Strength of Coy 11 offs 145 O.R. 3 Field Amb.	Appx [sig]
Reserve Billets ZELOBES	20/5/14		A fine day, very warm. Observer balloon near camp was shelled during evening. O E Coy & Lt Hartley to Hd Qrs 145 Coy at LAVEME found the town evacuated owing to hostile shelling anticipated. A quiet uneventful 24 hours. Sick Nil Casualties Nil. Strength of Company 11 offs 145 O.R. Reserve (2 Field Amb)	Appx [sig]

WAR DIARY

INTELLIGENCE SUMMARY

Army Form C. 2118.

Page 30

of **199 MACHINE GUN COMPANY**

for **MAY 1914.**

Place	Date	Hour	Summary of Events and Information	Remarks and references to Appendices
RESERVE BILLETS ZELOBES.	21/5/14		A fine day. Very hot. O.C. Coy to Hd.Qrs. 116 M.G. Coy at LAVENTIE re relief. Reconnoitred line FAUQUISSART SECTOR. No 2 Section moved from ZELOBES during afternoon to LAVENTIE to relieve a section of 116 M.G. Coy. Remainder of Coy will go to ZELOBES on relief. Relief completed by 11 p.m. A very busy day. Section overhauling gear & getting ready for line. A quiet uneventful 24 hours on area. Sick Nil. Casualties Nil. Strength of Company 11 Off. (1 S.R.) 145 O.R. 3 Field Amb.	[signature]
TRENCHES FAUQUISSART SECTOR	22/5/14		A very wet afternoon, cleared up during the afternoon. The Company relieved the 116 Bng. M.G. Coy in the trenches in FAUQUISSART Sector, becoming attached to the 116 Bng. 3 Section in the trenches, No. 3, 2 & 4 Sections in the line on Right, Centre & Left respectively. No 1 Section was relieved as MERVILLE by a section of the Coy & proceed to LAVENTIE arriving at 2 p.m. Coy Hd.Qrs. allocated in LAVENTIE. Transport to LAVENTIE-LA GORGUE ROAD. Relief completed by 12 noon. O.C. Coy attended a Conference at Hd. of Bng Sect. Quarters during the afternoon. Received 13 Reinforcement from Base 2 Gunners both being Scotchmen were posted to No 3 Section. Pte Briggs & L.C. Osborne rejoined Company from Corps Rest Station. A quiet uneventful 24 hours. Sick 1. Pte Jones to C.C.S. Strength of Company according to casualty list. Strength of Coy 11 Off. (1 S.R.) 145 other ORs. Gun front 4,500 Rds on hostile hide areas during the night.	[signature]
TRENCHES FAUQUISSART SECTOR	23/5/14		A fine day, warm & bright. Aerial activity throughout day. On 2 occasions hostile planes attempted to cross our line at a low altitude but were driven by Lt Gns out AA fire. O.C. Coy visited Sect No. 9 of all sections on the line found all correct, carried a ranging from Frogmouth & Culled at Bng Hd.Qrs. during evening. Pte Roberts returned to duty from Corps Rest Station. A quiet uneventful 24 hours. Gun front 5,500 fire on hostile areas during night. No retaliation from enemy. Sick Nil. Casualties Nil. Strength of Coy 11 Off. (1 A.O. 1) 145 other Ranks. (H.A. (NZ))	[signature]
TRENCHES FAUQUISSART SECTOR	24/5/14		A fine day, bright & warm. Received section to Baths during forenoon. O.C. Coy to Trenches C of R section during forenoon, visited all gun places, carried alterations & improvements necessary. O.C. Coy to Bng during afternoon re gas operation. Arranged for Co-operation with M.G. fire. No change during the night. Gas apparatus about hostile relief was taken place. Between 10 pm & 1 am guns were engaged all areas over which relief known to pass. O.C. Coy to line during night. Sect returned at 1 am. A Portuguese on the 21st now holds the right Sect. of Bng front. A quiet 24 hours. Every Coy quiet. Sick Nil. Casualties Nil. Strength of Coy 11 Off. (1 S.R.) 145 Other Rks. (1 officer Sick on C.C.S.)	[signature]
TRENCHES FAUQUISSART SECTOR	25/5/14		A fine day, warm & bright. Aerial activity during forenoon, several hostile planes attempted to cross our line at a low altitude but were driven off by M.G. fire from A.A. posts. Transport & Hd. Qrs. to Baths during afternoon. A quiet 24 hours on the front. O.C. Coy to ZELOBES during evening to see O.C. 116 Bng. Guns from 4,500 Rds on hostile hide areas during night. Sick Nil. Casualties Nil. Strength of Coy 11 Off (1 S.R.) 145 other Ranks.	[signature]

Page 34.

WAR DIARY of **199. MACHINE GUN COMPANY**

INTELLIGENCE SUMMARY

for **MAY 1914**.

Army Form C. 2118.

Place	Date	Hour	Summary of Events and Information	Remarks and references to Appendices
TRENCHES. FAUQUISSART SECTOR	26/5/14		A fine day, very warm & bright. Aerial activity throughout day, good results attained by M.G's against hostile planes attempting to fly low over our lines. O.C Coy & Lt Asquith to Trenches hill (Conductor Sector) to reconnoitre for positions for forward. Preparations for forthcoming operations continued. During the night 240 Alarm was received from front line. Gas curtain taken down, no gas noticeable. Gun fire 4000 Rds on to hostile back areas during night. Sick One. Pte Archer to 1st E. to & thence to C.E.S Shinele ab Strength accordingly to casualty N.L. Strength of Company 11 officers 149 O.R. (1 Offr Sick)	Appendx
TRENCHES FAUQUISSART SECTOR	27/5/14		A fine day, very warm & bright. Aerial activity during forenoon. M.G's successful in keeping enemy planes from flying at a low altitude. O.C Coy carried out a further reconnaissance of front line returning to HQ Coys at 3 pm. Sections to HQ, No 4 Coy. No 4 Sections were relieved on the 7 members by No 1 Section during forenoon. Relief completed without incident by 11 AM. Guns fire 5000 Rds on hostile back areas during the night. A quiet, uneventful 24 hours. Sick No. 2. Vorcoulie N.L. Strength of Coy 11 Offr 148 OR. (1 Offr Sick)	Appendx
TRENCHES FAUQUISSART SECTOR	28/5/14		A fine day, warm & bright. O.C Coy to Front line for Reconnaissance of DEVIL'S JUMP & TRIVELET, noting No 3 section new Sites. Reserve section to Baths. & made ready for O.C Coy during evening. A quiet uneventful 24 hours. Guns fire 4,500 Rds on to hostile back area during night. Sick No. Covailliv N.L. Strength of Coy 11 Offr. (1 Sick) 149 O.R.	Appendx
TRENCHES. FAUQUISSART SECTOR	29/5/14		A fine day, very warm, but dull. Slight rain during afternoon. Reserve section on C.O's inspection during forenoon. O.C Coy to HQ G.II Bde & P.Bre during afternoon. Returns to HQ Coy the No 1 Coy at Streass. A quiet uneventful day tonight. Guns fired 5000 Rds on hostile back areas during night. Sick 2. Pte Noble E.C.E.S. Sick (Mumps) through R.E. & thence to 1st A from Trenches Escrinelles. N.L. Strength of Company 11 Offr. (Sick) 148 Other Ranks. (1 Field Amb.)	Appendx
TRENCHES FAUQUISSART SECTOR	30/5/14		A fine day. No 4 section relieved No 2 section on left of Coy areas during forenoon. No 2 Section to Baths during afternoon about relief action during morning against a bath near Coy HQ. Reserve section front carryon parties for R.E during the night. 1 other was notified to Coy by Special Letter R.E. and Returns & fuel. Guns fired 5000 Rds during the night - co-op each with (Sick) 145 other Ranks. (1 Held Ambulance)	Appendx
	31-5-14	2 Total		

Munkly Capt.

Commanding 199 M.G Company

SECRET.

WAR DIARY.

OF

199th Machine Gun Coy.

FOR

June 1917.

Page 38

WAR DIARY
INTELLIGENCE SUMMARY
of 199 MACHINE GUN COMPANY
for JUNE 1919

Army Form C. 2118.

(Erase heading not required.)

Place	Date	Hour	Summary of Events and Information	Remarks and references to Appendices
Trenches FAUQUISSART SECTOR	31/5/19		A fine day. Reports below to have worked part during day, preparing indirect fire positions. 1st HARTLEY to 18AM MG Battery at Knyeh Grounds, after LINDSEY attended a Coalhole of WHITELAND. 6.15 Am to have discovered Invisibility defective. Moved Battn Overcoats Gun from FOOKS LODGE to another position. PT SMITH attacked Ammd dump by duty. A tiring night Artillery action on both sides. the Coy carried out a small raid from Neuve Chapelle during the night. Guns fired 5558 Rds. Hostile Shell fire been very heavy. According to reports from prisoners who M.G. fire has been deadly accurate & worry them. a Lt. Sgt N.D. Consultanth Strength of Coy 11 Offrs (1 Sick) 143 O.R. (NLR/a b). The month has been one of exceptional instructional value, the company has that several moves & carried out several raids as short notice. It has now had a good practical experience in all their sections & the Sub-sections have quickly adapted itself to the various conditions & variations of each. The lesson of the Company has been magnificent, they had no casualties. The enemy, so far as can be ascertained, was quite considerable. The value of the Ant average assisted fire was realised as a great deal of indirect night firing was carried out. The values of the Anti aircraft was enthusiastically attempted. Work consists of instruction which brought to notice by the actions attained in driving hostile planes back will attempt to fly towards our front areas.	
TRENCHES FAUQUISSART SECTOR	1/6/19		Roll of Officers on Strength of Company on 1st June 1919. Company Capt. J. McHUGH, M.C. Lieut C.W. PORTER 2/Lieut R.M. THOMAS 2/Lt B.B. ADAM " R. ELSON Lt. W.F. THORPE Company Sgt Major S. NORTHERN. A fine day. Reserve section to Baths. Carried out during day O.C. Coy Inspected transport during from G. Wallace to Lute Ant. Sect. Pt. BROWN & L.A. sick turn of the enemy, an of our observation balloons was attacked & burnt by hostile aircraft. Gun fired 800 Rds during night on to hostile trench areas. A quiet remainder 2-4 hours. O.C. Coy visited all sections in the live during this night, & found all correct & alert. Str 2 Casualty Nil. Strength of Company 11 Officers (1 Sick) 143 Other Ranks (2 Field Amt.) Comdg Coy 5th C.E.S. Commdg A Section " C " Sub Sect Off E " Transport M/Str. Coy Qr Ms Sgt Lieut R.J. HARTLEY, S. ASQUITH 2/Lt N.P. BARKER " A.E. LINDLEY " T.B. FRANCIS J.H. BALLIWELL B/m Command. Commdg B. Section Sub Sect Off. A. Section Commdg D Section Sub Sect Off D Section	

PAGE 30.

WAR DIARY of **199 MACHINE GUN COMPANY**

INTELLIGENCE SUMMARY for **JUNE 1914**

Army Form C. 2118.

Place	Date	Hour	Summary of Events and Information	Remarks and references to Appendices
TRENCHES FAUQUISSART SECTOR	2/6/14		A fine day, warm & bright. Aerial activities on both sides during day. Reserve section on C.O's Inspection during morning. A very good turnout. Pte Edwards yd. gd. has leave to United Kingdom from 3rd to 13th June. O.C. Coy & Lt. Hartly to Gelebes during afternoon to arrange relief by 146 M.G. Coy. Artillery on both sides very active throughout. White night. M.Gs fired 6500 Rds on Hostile back areas during the night. Otherwise a quiet uneventful 24 hours. Sick NIL. Fauquillin NIL. Strength of Company 11 Off (5 sick) 143 other Ranks (2 sick inclusive)	Appxt
TRENCHES FAUQUISSART SECTOR	3/6/14		A fine day, cursid activities throughout the day. No 2 section left Laventie for Robecq at 8 am, in relief of a section of 146 M.G. Coy who take their place in Coy Reserve arriving at 5 pm. On arrival at Robecq a cut section had to proceed to Trelignies near Aire to take over similar duties, being replaced at Robecq by night with German Machine guns fired 1,500 Rds during the night on hostile back areas. (Pte Beecom from of Leb bat to C.C.S. Shuve off.) Strength Sick NIL Strength of Coy 11 Off, 142 other Ranks (14 A)	Appxt
TRENCHES FAUQUISSART SECTOR	4/6/14		A fine day. The Company was relieving in the Fauquissart sector of the line by the 146 M.G. Coy. Relief completed without incident by 1 pm. No 3 section relieved a section of 146 Coy at Merville for Current duties. No 3 Lt. Sections moved to Gelebes with Coy Hd Qrs. becoming flag in divisional reserve. Recruits 14 - Reinforcement from Bas Coy 1 Off & 30 O.Rs. Posted Coy t lt to B Offrs section 2 (private to No 2 section a quiet uneventful 24 hours. Sick NIL Fauquillis NIL. Strength of Company 11 Off (5 Sick) 146 other Ranks (14 A)	Appxt
DIVISIONAL RESERVE BILLETS GELEBES	5/6/14		A fine day, very warm, double plans and bullets burn during morning. O.C. Coy to Robecq visiting No 2 section during evening. A quiet uneventful 24 hours. Reserve Section cleaning equipment & gear during day. Sick NIL, Fauquillis NIL. Strength of Coy 11 Off, 146 other Ranks (1 sick)	Appxt
DIVISIONAL RESERVE BILLETS GELEBES	6/6/14		A fine day, Very warm. Reserve sections on Parade for Inspection. O.C. Coy to Merville visiting No 3 Section saw 42 O.R's who is getting quite well. Returned to Coy Hd Qrs at 3 pm. Rain during evening. Reidonn rode over from Merville & reported that Pte Webb had been accidentally drowned in the River Lays, whilst getting a day fracas overnette, the first death in the Company, since its arrival in France. Sick NIL, Fauquillis NIL, Strength of Coy 11 Off (1 Sick) 145 other Ranks. A quiet uneventful 24 hours in the line.	Appxt

Army Form C. 2118.

WAR DIARY of 199 MACHINE GUN COMPANY

INTELLIGENCE SUMMARY

(Erase heading not required.)

for JUNE 1917.

Instructions regarding War Diaries and Intelligence Summaries are contained in F. S. Regs., Part II. and the Staff Manual respectively. Title Pages will be prepared in manuscript.

Place	Date	Hour	Summary of Events and Information	Remarks and references to Appendices
Warnimont Baraque Huts 2 Hebba	7/6/17		A fine afternoon, bright & warm. A heavy storm during the night. Capt Mahley proceeded on leave to U.K. Command of Company assumed by Capt Bartlett accompanied by No 2 Section. Pte Webb buried at Merville at 2pm. A quiet uneventful 24 hours. Sick nil. Casualties Nil. Strength of Coy 11 Offr (1 Sick) 145 OR. (1 at A.)	forecast
—do—	8/6/17		A fine day, bright & warm. Lt Hartley proceeded to Merville during the forenoon to conduct the board of enquiry re/ght death of Pte Webb. Lt Portis discharged from hospital rejoins Company. Reserve section at Zelote practiced rapid wastage movements during a mimic Bois Boken attack. The civilians was again shown the track, as admitted to Field Ambulance. Improvements carried out at Bullek & Cookhouse & meatsafe built. A quiet uneventful 24 hours. Sick nil. Casualties Nil. Strength of Coy 11 Offr 145 OR 2 Field Ambulance	forecast
—do—	9/6/17		A fine day, bright & warm. Aerial activity throughout day. Lt Hartley to Rotrech to visit No 2 Section. Found all correct. Cattle all changed to day though got each & pads company got company out the day. Selected teams & drivers for the show, & preparations for same begun. Reserve section at renewed arms gloom were & gas drill during day. A quiet uneventful 24 hours. Sick nil. One Pte Johnson to C.C.S & struck off Strength accordingly. One Pte Johnson to F.A. Casualties 11 Offr 144 OR.	forecast
—do—	10/6/17		A fine day. Sections inspected in Marching order, a good turn out. Gun drawing during remainder of day. Sgt Matthews appointed C.Q.M. Sgt of 99 m.g Coy. A quiet uneventful 24 hours. Improvements carried out in Bullek during stores of occupation. Sick nil. Casualties Nil. Strength of Company 11 Offrs 144 Other Ranks. (2 Field Ambulance)	forecast
—do—	11/6/17		A hot day. Sultry & Dull. Rain during forenoon, cleared got cool in the evening. Sgt Matthews left for Beautie to join 99 M.G. Coy on promotion. Section carried out training of new wasp pistol. During the day No 1 section carried out an experiment with the queen pack. It was found unsatisfactory (for carrying BELT Boxes) perhaps due to the lack of men experienced & trained in the methods of pack, also of service this allowing limited transport attack, the carriages of them on the line of march would be an objection to their issue to Machine Gun Companies. A cookhouse & oven built in the Transport lines & also in Coy 11 Offr 143 Other Ranks (2 Field Ambulance)	forecast
—do—	12/6/17		A fine day. Section continued training. O.C Coy to Batt Qrs 14 & July Regt re attaching a section to the Batt for a special purpose to tomorrow late. Sgt Heath to section sgt of No 3 section vice Matthews. O.C Coy to Merville re inspection, found all correct. A very quiet 24 hours. Four very quiet, sick nil. 6 casualties Nil. Strength of Company 11 Officers 143 Other Ranks (2 Field Ambulance)	forecast

2449 Wt. W14957/Mgo 750,000 1/16 J.B.C. & A. Forms/C.2118/12.

Page 41.

WAR DIARY
of N° 199 MACHINE GUN COMPANY
INTELLIGENCE SUMMARY
(Erase heading not required.) for JUNE 1914

Army Form C. 2118.

Place	Date	Hour	Summary of Events and Information	Remarks and references to Appendices
DIVISIONAL RESERVE BILLETS ZELOBES	13/6/14		A fine day. Received orders that the Section on Anti Aircraft duty bb the 154th M.G. Coy to be withdrawn to Coy Hd Qrs at Zelobes being relieved on A-A duty by the 154th M.G. Battery on the instruction of O.C Coy to be on its way to 152nd M.G. Coy when to report to 152nd O.C Coy to arrange details of relief by section. Details of Relief arranged. On Return to Coy Hd Qtr found orders awaiting that 2 Sections were to proceed to Steenwerck reporting to 2nd Army M.G. Officer, N°s 1 & 4 Sections were detailed for this duty & left Zelobes under orders of O.C 140 Machine Gun Company at 5pm on way to Steenwerck, met by an officer of 140 Coy who stated they were not required until the 15th inst whereon they returned to Coy Hd Qrs during afternoon receiving further orders for Section to report to 2nd Army under command of O.C 11th M.G. Coy at LAVENTIE on 14th inst. Bill relief arranged by evening. A very quiet day. Situation during 24 hours quiet. Sick N. Casualties N. Strength by day 11 offs & 143 other Ranks. (2 Field Amb)	(appendix)
DIVISIONAL RESERVE BILLETS ZELOBES	14/6/14		A fine day. N°1 Section left Zelobes at 8am proceeded to Steenbecq for duties with 140 M.G. Coy. N°4 Section at 10am proceeded to Steenwerck for duty with 140 M.G. Coy. N°2 Section on relief arrived at Zelobes at 1pm had dinner & then to Steenbecq for duty with 140 M.G. Coy. Distribution of Coy at 6pm was as follows. Coy Hd Qrs at Zelobes. N°s 1 & 2 Section at Steenbecq N°4 Section at Merville. 1A Section also. The division received an M.G. escort from the day the divisional train was held up between Strazeele & Limber Chennont 4 Thorps & mules were lost, but extra were limited to one horse for Officers. 3 mules the only mules in the Company. The Limber & Teams were turned out indeed. The ground although in a composer position they could not compete against horses not appeared to show also a great success, some Thorpy some Chennont being brought to notice. Especially the condition of animals. Received 15th Reinforcement from Base (5 gunners) including Pte Archer. Temporary posted to gunner 1 to N° Section. Pte Burke to Coy Hd Qrs as N.R duty. Situation very quiet & very cuny 24 hours. all ranks complete as to 4 pm Sick N. Casualties N. Strength by Company 11 officers 148 other Ranks (2 Field Amb)	(appendix)
Reserve Billets Zelobes	15/6/14		A fine day bright & warm. At 11am orders were received to concentrate the company at Zelobes. All Sections were withdrawn from their respective areas & the company was assembled complete at Zelobes by 3pm. Orders were received for the company to relieve the 114 M.G. Coy on the Ferme du Bois Sector on the 16th inst. O.C Coy to Coy Hd Qrs by Coy to tour Pt to arrange relief. A quiet 24 hours. Casualties & men in good condition ready for anything. Sick N. Casualties N. Strength by day 11 Offs 148 other Ranks. (2 Field Amb)	(appendix)
DIVISIONAL RESERVE BILLETS ZELOBES	16/6/14		A fine day. Very hot. Coy relieved 114 M.G. Coy in the Ferme du Bois Section dispositions as follows. 3 Sections i.e Lay Float N°s N°1 on flight, N°2 in Centre, N°3 on Left. N°4 in Coy Reserve at Le Tourret. Coy Hd Qrs & transport at Le Tourret. Relief completed by 8.30 a.m. As present the coy was so attached to the 1st Brigade Portuguese expeditionary force. O.C Coy to Portg Hd Qrs at 2 p.m. saw Brigadier & Interpreter & explained dispositions to him & holding the Ferme du Bois Sector. Allay at present and at 11:30 Patrols on hostile C.Ts & Saps were sent during the night. Situation to show a quiet uneventful 24 hours. Enemy fired 25 ORs Rounds on positions. Sick N. Casualties N. Strength by Company 11 Offs 148 other Ranks. (3 field Amb)	(appendix)

PAGE 42.

WAR DIARY of 199 MACHINE GUN COMPANY

Army Form C. 2118.

INTELLIGENCE SUMMARY

for JUNE 1914.

(Erase heading not required.)

Instructions regarding War Diaries and Intelligence Summaries are contained in F.S. Regs., Part II. and the Staff Manual respectively. Title Pages will be prepared in manuscript.

Place	Date	Hour	Summary of Events and Information	Remarks and references to Appendices
Trenches Fme du Bois Sector	17/6/14		A fine day, very hot. O.C. Coy visited all sections in the line. Altered dispositions of defence of guns at Range X & Samson Post. Saw Batt. Commdr. 21st P. 9-19 & arranged for Bombing Posts to come under orders of Team Commdrs., also arranged for co-operation with 1M Battery (144) left Section Hd Qrs at POHF Loop. shelled during the night, much damage but no casualties. Guns fire 3000 Rds on hostile track area during the night, a great unsuccessful 24 hours. Sick 0 or. B.s. Hosp. to hospital Casualties NiL. Strength of Company 11 officers 148 other Ranks. (3 field Ambulance)	Mcdt
Trenches Fme du Bois Sector	18/6/14		A fine day, very hot & dry. Loy Sgt Major granted leaves to U.K. Reserve Section busy rebuilding & repairing the lille post which he returned to duty from C.R.S. at quiet day on the line. Section settled down & all defences running well. Guns fired 5000 Rds on hostile track areas during the night. A quiet unsuccessful 24 hours. Sick 11 offrs. 148 other Ranks. (3rd fd. Amb)	Mcdt
Trenches Fme du Bois Sector	19/6/14		A fine day, very hot & bright. Aerial activity throughout the day. Hostile artillery active against Richebourg St Vaast, drew hvy Capt Murray returned from leave & re-assumed command of the Sector from Colonel Pittoulaid. No officer men looking over Pt. Summhr. returned from 1st Army Rest Camp, & delegates to 1st Army Rest Camp. Guns fired 6000 Rds on hostile track area during the night. Sick NiL Casualties NiL, a quiet unsuccessful 24 hours. Strength of Company 11 Offrs 148 other Ranks. (3 field Ambulance)	Mcdt
Trenches Fme du Bois Sector	20/6/14		A fine day, warm & bright. O.E. Coy to Sms. Visited all guns & sections HdQrs, also visited all Coy & Section Hd Qrs, also visited Nº 3 Section relieved Nº4 Section in the sup section to implement Relief. Relief completed without incident by 8.30 am. O.C. Coy to Bnry Hd Qrs 1st Portuguese Bnry drew officers to saw Brigadier & explained defence scheme to him to Hanley & Davies to Bephmst during afternoon to interview the Selection officer Royal flying Corps. Slight hostile artillery against Richebourg St Vaast action during day. M.Gs fired 5000 Rds on hostile track areas during the night. A quiet uneventful 24 hours. Sick Nil, Casualties Nil, Strength of Coy 11 Offr 148 other Rks. (3 fd amb)	Mcdt
Trenches Fme de Bois Sector	21/6/14		A fine day, very cool & bright. Inspection of Billets & mule lines by C.O during forenoon. Nc.E. Nichols reported from C.R.S. Received 16th Reinforcement from Base (5 gunners) posted to Nº1 section. O.E. Coy to Hd. Qrs. 1st Portc guese Brigade made arrangements for co-operation in raid by 148 Inf (3 Brigade) 16th Bnion. On out night return by 2nd Lieuts 6 & Inf Retg team on our right in the further Sector. Guns fired 4000 Rounds on hostile track area during the night. Also operations both flash during night on the party on our right. The R.E. Party used the new gas projectiles Nello. Sick Nil, Casualties NiL, Strength of Company 11 Officers 180 o.R. (Pt Penny to C.C.S)	Mcdt

WAR DIARY of 199 MACHINE GUN COMPANY
INTELLIGENCE SUMMARY
for JUNE 1914

Army Form C. 2118.

PAGE N°. 3.

Place	Date	Hour	Summary of Events and Information	Remarks and references to Appendices
Trenches Fme du Bois Sector	22/6/14		A fine day, cool, rain during afternoon. Reserve Section to Baths at VIEILLE CHAPELLE. O.C. Coy to Hd Qrs 1st Brigade P.E.F. to arrange co-operation in Artillery action by P.E.F. & upon the Portuguese artillery against hostile area of BOARS HEAD. M.Gs co-operated bringing indirect T.s. & blumps firing 6000 Rds. Otherwise a quiet unventful 24 hours. Enemy very quiet. Pt H. HARRIS & Pt HOLE to C.C.S. Struck off strength accordingly. Sick N.L. Casualties N.L. Strength of Coy. 11 officers 199 O.R. (1 Field Ambulance).	present
Trenches Fme du Bois Sector	23/6/14		A fine day, cool & bright, rather windy during forenoon. Reserve Section inspected by C.O. Gas drill carried out during forenoon. Il trained to also time for reconnaissance. Lewis gun fire 6000 Rds during the night on to hostile back areas, otherwise a quiet unventful 24 hours, very little artillery activity. Sick N.L. Casualties N.L. Strength of Company 11 officers 199 other Ranks (1 Field Ambulance).	present
Trenches Fme du Bois Sector	24/6/14		A fine day, bright & cool. Aerial activity throughout forenoon. N°.4 Section relieves N°.1 Section who left sector of Company area during the morning. Relief completed without incident by 8-15 a.m. W Battery to leave to U.K. Lt ASQUITH to report to 2/in Command vice Hartley to leave. Lt ADAMS & Pts Kt MERODLE during afternoon to obtain anti aircraft sights. A quiet unventful 24 hours. Guns in line fired 5000 Rds during night. Sick N.L. Casualties N.L. Strength of Company 11 Off. 144 Other Ranks. (1 Field Ambulance.)	present
Trenches Fme du Bois Sector	25/6/14		A fine day, very bright & cool. Aerial activity throughout day. Artillery quiet on sector. Reserve section to Baths during forenoon. Rain fell during evening & throughout the night. A very quiet unventful 24 hours quiet in whole sector area. Guns fired 6000 Rds on hostile back areas. Sick N.L. Casualties N.L. Strength of Company 11 Officers 144 other Ranks. (1 Field Ambulance).	present
Trenches Fme du Bois Sector	26/6/14		A fine day cool after the Rain. O.C. Coy to Ferry Hd Qrs 1st Portuguese Brig. Reserve Section experiment with system PARK — Pt ASQUITH to ASQUITH to be attd. at Coy H.Q. for Coy Emergency Bag. Jerry Improvements carried out on Brick, Cookhouse completed & meeting with Trenches. Co. quiet & unventful 24 hours. Lewis guns bore fire on hostile back areas during the night. Letrole avoid activity throughout the night. Sick R N.L. Casualties N.L. Strength of Coy. 11 Off. (1 Un) 144 O.R. (1 F.a.)	present

2449 Wt. W14957/M90 750,000 1/16 J.B.C. & A. Forms/C.2118/12.

PAGE 4H

WAR DIARY of No 199 MACHINE GUN COMPANY
INTELLIGENCE SUMMARY
for JUNE 1914

Army Form C. 2118.

Place	Date	Hour	Summary of Events and Information	Remarks and references to Appendices
TRENCHES Mc du Bois Sector	27/6/19		A fine day, not Rain down early hours of morning. Inspection of No 1 Section by C.O. Previous to going into the trenches. A quiet uneventful 24 hours. During the night fires & explosions with a rattling M.G. schroots. Workers with from the Germ's. It hirts. Into 8000 Rds on to front line area, also 6000 Rds un-co-op eration with artillery. Programme of Portugueze artillery. Sub No 1 Boismille No Strength of day 11 Offs 149 ORs (1 F.A)	[signature]
TRENCHES Me du Bois Sector	28/6/19		A fine day. No 1 Section relieves No 2 Section in trenches. Relief completed by 8.30 am without incident. C.O. to Carriers trevies demonstration of M.G. fire carried out by Canadian M.M.G. Battery. Commenced at 8am during absence of C.O., O.C. Coy. (Hunmaker) attacked from 8N/S Rd. R Edwards 90 to Trench Side placed on P.B's & deposits for baths. Struck off through overrunning. Strength of day 11 Offs 148 Othr Rnks (2 F.A) A quiet uneventful 24 hours. Sick 2. Casualties Nil	[signature]
TRENCHES Me du Bois Sector	29/6/19		A fine day, Reserve Section to Baths. Old Qrs. No 2 Section & Transport to Divisional delay for Gas. 15 gas through Gas (No O.R). Test satisfactory. Fc day burst 4 Dewar R? to Fields Amb Sick. A quiet uneventful 24 hrs. Sem fires 6000 Rds on to hostile held areas. Sick 2. Boismille Nil. Strength of Company 11 Offs 148 Othr Rnks. (4 Field Ambulances)	[signature]

[signature] Capt
Commanding 199 Machine Gun Coy

In the field
30-6-14

Vol 8

War Diary.

199. M G Coy

July 1917

WAR DIARY

Page N° 5.

Army Form C. 2118.

199 MACHINE GUN COMPANY

for JULY 1919

Place	Date	Hour	Summary of Events and Information	Remarks and references to Appendices
TRENCHES Fme des Pres SECTOR	30/7/19		A fair day, dull & overcast. Rain during intervening nights. O.C. Coy returned from reading, creeping barrage fire of Machine Guns at CAMIERS, & re assumed command of the Company. C.S. Major returned from leave during the day. Pte Regt. to leave to U.K. A very quiet uneventful 24 hours. Guns fired 4000 rds on hostile back areas during the night. Sect N4, 0.connallie N.W. strength of Coy, 11 officers 148 Other Ranks (4 Field Ambulance). Taking a retrospect of the month, it has been another fairly quiet & uneventful month. The Company has spent a time in each sector of the Divisional Front & gained a most valuable knowledge of all three sectors. The training the personnel has been able to carry out has been quite satisfactory. The frequent short moves we the move from one area to another has been a great advantage. Moreover the much value of the Company a great deal. The Casualties of the Company have again been very light & the sick wastage is Valuable experience has been gained in the various minor operations carried out & while much information what hostile, back against the different sectors of the Divisional Front. During the latter part of the month the Company has been associated exclusively with the 1st Portugls. & the Portugese Expert troops, who's Valuable information regarding the personnel of that force has been obtained.	(signature)
			Officers on Strength of Company on 1/7/19 Capt. J. MUNEIS. M.C. Commanding Company Lieut R.J. HARTLEY. 2/in command (on leave U.K) Lieut G. ASQUITH. " A Section — E.W. PORTER. Commanding A Section 2/Lieut D.B. ADAM " B Section 2/Lieut A.E. LINDLEY. — B " Lieut R. ELSON Sub Section Off A Section — W.P. BARKER Sub Section Off B " 2/Lt RM THOMAS " " C " — T.B. FRANCIS " " C " Lieut W.F. THORPE Transport Offr & Qr. Master. Coy Sgt. Major S. NORTHERN. Coy Qr Mr Sgt. J.H BALKWELL	
ABERTURES (MC du Bois) SECTOR	1/7/19		A fair day, dull & overcast. Reserve Section inspected by C.O during afternoon. During the night guns in Sn/4 carried out a co-operating operation in conjunction with a bombardment by the Portugues Artillery During the night 9,500 rds were fired on hostile back areas. Admits in quiet & uneventful 24 hours Sector Ossoulles hill. Strength of Company 11 officers. 148 other Ranks (4 Field Ambulance)	(signature)

WAR DIARY of 199th MACHINE GUN COMPANY

Army Form C. 2118.

INTELLIGENCE SUMMARY

PAGE No 16

Month: **JULY 1914** [sic – likely 1918]

Place	Date	Hour	Summary of Events and Information	Remarks and references to Appendices
TRENCHES Fme du Bois SECTOR	2/7/14		A fine day, very bright aeros activity throughout day. No 2 Section relieved No 3 Section in left section of Company front during forenoon. Relief completed without incident by 11 am. At Pt.PK to line our Rearmaments at 1 pm the Portuguese battery behind EDWARDS Road suddenly opened fire. 3 shells fell on to one of our emplacements in the 15 min unfortunately killing Pte PARROTT & wounding Pte BAKER. Report on occurrence was rendered both to Bn HQ & to 1st Portuguese Brigade. During the night a heavy bombardment twice cut the whole front emplacemts the Post Box Fme & the hostile shelling lasted 1½ hours during which time the hostile infantry attempted to raid our trenches opposite Neuve Chapelle, with which success no not get known. The Sections on the line however were both involved. M.G.s in line were in action, putting quite an effective rattage out & no NoMansLand. Strength of Company 11 offrs 149 other Ranks (+ 2 Field Ambulances)	[sig]
TRENCHES Fme du Bois SECTOR	3/7/14		A fine day, very warm. Presents section to Bths Pte Parrott buried in St.Vaast Cemetery. O.C. Coy visited all gun positions between 2 & 4 pm & found all correct. A quiet day, our guns active against hostile lines throughout day. Pte – presumably in retaliation for the hostile raid of the previous night, Pte Edwards 90 & Davies 76 can carry on. Strength. Offr Strength recently. A quiet unsuccessful 24 hour Guns 1st 5,200 RdsBn k.o.d.R.B./R.H. Sec Hill Howitzers Av. Strength of Coy 11 off 143 Other Ranks (+ field ambulance)	[sig]
TRENCHES Fme du Bois SECTOR	4/7/14		A dull day, very close, rain during forenoon. Recent selection to see Demonstration during forenoon & to Bths in afternoon. A quiet uneventful day. O.C. Coy to tng establishment New M.G. Emplacements they will be ready in about a week. Some hostile artillery action against Regts and sector during the evening, but nothing developed. Enemy in his front lines SJF Hill. Bde lines Coal Company 11 officers 143 other Ranks (2 Field Ambulance)	[sig]
TRENCHES Fme du Bois SECTOR	5/7/14		A cool day, rather dull. O.C. Coy to Brigade Hd Qrs to meet Commdr 1st & 2nd M.G. Squadrons Portuguese in forming up. Defects No 3 Section during evening. Presents to gang met, due, found them & dismiss very satisfy. A quiet uneventful 24 hours. Buns on line Bty Pst 6000 Rds during night in haul back area, Bde, N/L Strength of Company 11 officers 143 other Ranks (2 Field Ambulance)	[sig]
TRENCHES Fme du Bois SECTOR	6/7/14		A fine day, bright & warm. Aerial activity throughout day. Adverse hostile activity against Portuguese positions in area to Aaquinte & QMS Balkwell to leave U.K. 6.G.Coy to bring his Coy into Relief by No 1 Squadron M.G.S. returned at 12 noon. No 3 Section relieved No 4 Section in right sector during morning Relief completed without incident by 9.30 a.m. Worked by B.M.G.O. 2nd Bns during afternoon, re-co-operation with Brigade on right. Pte O.C. Coy 8th M.G. Coy at Butte taking enemy. Pte Carp returned to Duty from Field Ambs. A quiet uneventful 24 hours. Continue to experiments the night we expect Lieut-Col Rowsell's Fd. Str.gth of Company 11 offers 143 Other Ranks (2 Field Amb.)	[sig]

2449 Wt. W14957/Mop 750,000 1/16 J.B.C.& A. Forms/C2118/12

WAR DIARY

199 MACHINE GUN COMPANY

INTELLIGENCE SUMMARY

July 1914

Army Form C.2118.

Place	Date	Hour	Summary of Events and Information	Remarks and references to Appendices
TACTICALS Fme du Bois SECTOR	7/7/17		A fine day, very bright & warm. Aerial activity throughout the day. Hostile artillery fairly active during the forenoon. Reserve lecture postponed during forenoon, trouble postponed during afternoon. O.C. Coy visited O.C. No 1 M.G. Squadron re reliefs, came to centre of with him proceeded round all Strongpoints on the line & visited by D.M.G.O. during afternoon. Lt Penny returned to duty from C.C.S. Sgt Matthews promoted W.O. Class II & posted as 1st Reserve & No 10 M.G. Gunner as 2nd Reserve during the evening & found all quiet. Nothing during the night. Strength of Coy 4 offrs 141 O.Rs. A quiet day. O.C. Coy visited Coy he H.Q.s during the evening. Strength of Coy 4 offrs 141 O.Rs. (1 Field Ambulance) During the afternoon an aeroplane W.S.M.G.A. strength of Coy 11 offrs 141 O.Rs. (1 Field Ambulance) During the afternoon an aeroplane SWR Rd. Casualties Nil. Strength of Coy 11 offrs 141 O.Rs. Cavalry on the front of the 16 Bde on our right. It lasted all night & heavy bombardment was begun by the enemy. Chiefly on the front of the 16 Bde on our right. was energetically continued till midnight the hostile lines about the PARABOLA during the night, 8,500 Rds. 3 guns of the light Section exploited the hostile lines about the PARABOLA during the night, 8,500 Rds. being fired, however the enemy made no any attempted infantry operations	Appendix
TRENCHES Fme du Bois SECTOR	8/7/17		A dull day, cool & overcast. Reserve lecture to Baker during afternoon/ Sgt Matthew to 10 Base Shorthand/ The hostile batteries of the previous night were steadily normal, attempt to obtain an observation regarding the fault of their Withdrew Montagny & 62nd Anti Aircraft during about the Zeemt du Boio. Along to the rest of the M.G. Batteries of the Batts were. The fine Gun Zone Rds needed burst to obtain an enemy rifle and line. A quiet evening and 24 hours. Enemy activity 10 offrs 143 other Ranks (GHQ) during the night on to hostile Bosch areas 8th RHA Casualties Nil. Strength of Coy 11 offrs 143 other Ranks (GHQ)	Appendix
TRENCHES Fme du Bois SECTOR	9/7/17		A fine day, cool & pleasant, too dull Aerial work tactile artillery activity during forenoon as counter battery work. Visited by O.C. No 1 M.G. Sqdn. & final details of relief arranged in theatre to be given to see BARROW Bn CO & officer. A quiet morning. Dr James on the line. Sea aeroplanes were seen by No Coy RE during the night. New hostile batteries from the enemy guns fired 4000 Rds during the night on to hostile Bosch areas 8th RHA Casualties Nil. Strength of Coy 11 offrs 148 (8 Bh Rev R)	Appendix
TRENCHES Fme du Bois SECTOR	10/7/17		A dull day, overcast, inclined to rain. Reserve lecture. Packing & cleaning up. Transport to start Quarter & Wheel Quarter at 12 M.G. Sqdn. arrived at 10 am & settled down. Coy Reliefs on the Zeemt du Bois Section by 1st M.E. Sqdn. Relief complete 12-15. A good march, 24 hours. Relieve to the Sub Coy Bombardier & Signalling for half brother Rifles (Act W)	Appendix
BILLETS LESTREM	11/7/17		Coy assembled at bivouac at 4 am. Bay. Company left to march by ROUGEMARE to VENOT by BETHUNE playing 9th Buffs relief L2/2 of 11 Buffs & settled down by 11-30 am. A quiet 24 hours. 14 Recn forwarded from Base point & 3 camp police 60 Bde 2 Lt rejoined. O/C Baker rejoined from C.C.S. Sgt Mal. To casualties. Nil Strength Company 11 officers (I was) 149 other Ranks (2 L & a	Appendix

2449 Wt. W14957/M90 750,000 1/16 J.B.C. & A. Forms/C.2118/12.

Army Form C. 2118.

PAGE 148

WAR DIARY of 199 MACHINE GUN COMPANY

INTELLIGENCE SUMMARY

for JULY 1914

(Erase heading not required.)

Instructions regarding War Diaries and Intelligence Summaries are contained in F. S. Regs., Part II. and the Staff Manual respectively. Title Pages will be prepared in manuscript.

Place	Date	Hour	Summary of Events and Information	Remarks and references to Appendices
VENDIN LEZ BETHUNE	13/7/14		A fine day, warm & bright. Sections scheduled gear & tackle during the day. Monthly M. Gun 118-Arty or Infantry. A quiet 24 hours. All sections given a lecture on antiaircraft duties during the day. Most of the sections had their photographs taken during the day & an officer group was also taken. Sick Nil Casualties Nil. Strength of Company 11 officers (3 heart) 144 Other Ranks (2 Field Ambulance)	Appendix
VENDIN LEZ BETHUNE	14/7/14		A fine day, warm & bright. All arrangements for entraining made. Company rested during the afternoon. A quiet day. At 10.15 pm Advance Party of Transport under command of Lieut Harvey left for the Station to entrain. Company Proceeded at 11-15 & marched to BETHUNE Station to Entrain. Reached Station Rendezvous at 12 m.d. Sick Nil Casualties Nil. Strength of Company 11 officers 144 Other Ranks. 2 Fields Ambulance. Pte Haghurst struck off strength to E.C.S. Station	Appendix
LEFFRINCKHOUCKE nr. DUNKERQUE	15/7/14		The entraining of the Company was completed by 1 am. Train left BETHUNE at 2.19 am & arrived DUNKERQUE at 12 noon. A quiet rum left. Company detrained complete & left by Route March for LEFFRINCK HOUCKE: a march of 5½ miles on partially drawn material & drawn. On arrival billets were obtained. Homes for the men, the Officers. Fairly wet weather. After noon received orders re "VOLUBLE" Company settled in Billets by 5 pm. A quiet afternoon & Night. New Registered Telephone address Cozeng of Company. Sick Nil Casualties Nil. Strength 11 officers (3 heart) 144 Other Ranks & 2 Field Ambulance.	Appendix
LEFFRINCKHOUCKE nr. DUNKERQUE	16/7/14		A fine day. Good breeze from sea during day. O.C. Coy Reported to M. Gm. 118 by Pony during afternoon. Company engaged scouring up ground throughout the day & Re-equipment from stores. A quiet & undisturbed 24 hours in billets. Sick Nil. Casualties Nil. Strength of Company 11 officers 146 Other Ranks	Appendix
LEFFRINCKHOUCKE nr. DUNKERQUE	17/7/14		A fine day, warm & bright. Company engaged during throughout forenoon in Rear shub during afternoon. Baths. O.E. Coy accompanied Beach to fire Rifle Range. Found Guard against ZUDCOTE BATTERY. Recd. an invitation that 2 Reinforcements will be arriving from East to Div before Battle. Sick Nil Casualties Nil. Strength of Company 11 officers 146 other Ranks (1 Field Ambulance)	Appendix
POST DUNKERQUE	18/7/14		A fine day. Company left LEFFRINCKHOUCKE under orders of the 6th Infy Brigade & proceeded to POST DUNKERQUE to Relieve Arrival after a wearying march along crowded roads at 4.30 pm. Reserve W. Harley. Had fixed up Posts. The Plants has a hot request for hostile shelling. All precautions taken. A quiet 24 hours. Pte Porter proceeded on leave this day. Sick Nil Casualties Nil. Strength of Company 11 officers (2 heart) 146 other Ranks (1½ 3 heart)	Appendix

PAGE 19

199th M.G. Coy

JULY 1917

Army Form C. 2118.

WAR DIARY
or
INTELLIGENCE SUMMARY

(Erase heading not required.)

Place	Date	Hour	Summary of Events and Information	Remarks and references to Appendices
NIEUPORT	18/7/17		A wet day. Major Shuli 144 Machine Gun Coy assumed command of the Company on the afternoon as 2 i/c of 199 M.G. Coy in the absence of Major Slough. At 2.30 H.Q. & Reserve Sect org. from Cap. Hurley's billet were moved to Lombardsyde tr 119 M.G.Coy to the NIEUPORT sector in light of 18/19th the Infantry 7 Sea aft reorganised the line during evening of the day who were compelled to 11 P.M. 2 officers casts on account of enemy shelling. We were liable to escape without casualties. Strength of Coy 11 Off (2 above) 176 other ranks (I.T.A.)	MTT Cox
	19/7/17		A dull day. During the morning the Germans made an attack on our front line positions. All our guns fired out on the S.O.S. Signal being put up a total of 12,500 rounds were fired by the 8 guns on the line during the hours of 2.30 & 10 A.M. One gun was blown up but luckily not seriously damaged the two teams working the guns were mowed & both fairly badly wounded. The Company came out of this their first general firing encounter very well indeed. I was very pleased with the behaviour of all ranks. 2/Lieut returned from Leave. Strength of Coy. 11 Off (2 above) 174 other ranks (I.T.A.)	MTT Cox
	20/7/17		A windy day. Lt. Asquith on his return from leave took over duties of 2nd i/c & remains at Transport lines in charge of the Reserve Sections. A barrage position was reconnoitred during the forenoon. Two emplacements were destroyed by hostile fire during the day. There were in favour of cheap d'issued orders for a gun to reach the gun position & side left to a new position as lock informed Owing to the dug out being practically demolished. Two new positions to reported from Basss & modification see of that Capn S. Bakwell is promoted W.O. Class II & is to report to 63 Coy. Strength of Coy. 11 Off (on leave) 146 O.R. (I.T.A)	MTT Cox

WAR DIARY / INTELLIGENCE SUMMARY

Army Form C. 2118.

199 M.G. Coy

JULY 1917

Page 50

Place	Date	Hour	Summary of Events and Information	Remarks and references to Appendices
NIEUPORT	21st		A fine bright day. Considerable aerial activity. The enemy's aircraft showed considerable activity. C.Q.M.S. Bathwell returned from leave & proceeded to join his new Company. Serjt J. Mutt not yet arrived. An enemy shell fell about 10.30 when the enemy commenced a heavy bombardment of our back areas using gas shells in large quantities.	
NIEUPORT	22nd		The enemy continued to use gas shells at intervals throughout the night. Our casualties consist to date of 1 Off. & 14 O.R. The effects of the gas do not appear to fully show themselves until 12 to 24 hours after the exposure to the gas. A fine day. Both considerable air activity. After a conference with the G.O.C. all guns were moved on to a new barrage line. Strength of Coy 11 Off. 115 O.R.	
-"-	23rd		Another fine day. Capt. Gaddoun appointed extra Captain to the Company & took charge Gas casualties now stand at 2 Off. & 6 O.R. No 4 Section came in for a slight bombardment during the day but suffered no casualties.	
-"-	24th		Rather a dull day & little aircraft activity. The enemy again employed gas shells during the night. Several heavy shells were dropped in the neighbourhood of Coy H.Q. Strength of Coy 11 Off. 115 O.R.	
-"-	25th		A dull morning with a little rain. Bright later to a fine afternoon. The C.O. went over to Bn H.Q. 4th G. Coy on our left to arrange communication with them. During early our own left group of guns opened on S.O.S lines firing 5000 rounds. Lieut S. Bailey returned to transport lines for a few days rest. Lt Asquith is now at Coy H.Q. acting 2nd in command.	

Page 51

WAR DIARY
or
INTELLIGENCE SUMMARY.
(Erase heading not required.)

Army Form C. 2118.

Place	Date	Hour	Summary of Events and Information	Remarks and references to Appendices
NIEUPORT	26		Bright day C.O. visited guns early in the morning + also inspected positions near REDAN to arrange to carry out a barrage between districts. Artillery of both sides very active shelled our gun positions + vicinity of the ISLAND being shelled unsuccessfully until 5pm. Casualties nil. Invited to carried out during night 3,000 rounds being fired at TOMBARTZYDE + vicinity of same.	MMZ Clark
"	27		Bright day Our positions all over + artillery of both sides very active especially during night. Special by A.C. came to TOMBARTZYDE Boulevard + bunks of the at 1.35 am + two M.G.'d the buoy were constructing wire posts of the Owing to unfavourable conditions operations were postponed. Fired 3,000 rounds indirect harassing fire during night. Our positions in the ISLAND seem to come in for particular attention from the enemy artillery + at present there is no appearance of our existence there.	HC
"	28		Bright day guns all covert, artillery still active attacking again having laid Gas on our ISLAND Position. R.E. bridgeheads for float to the night but no move began positions we find it necessary indirect fire. Guns again fired into NIEUPORT during night + but no for our casualties to be shelled.	MMP Clark

A534. Wt.W4473 M687 750,000 8/16 D.D.&L.Ltd. Forms/C.2118/13.

Army Form C. 2118.

WAR DIARY
or
INTELLIGENCE SUMMARY.
(Erase heading not required.)

Page 52

Place	Date	Hour	Summary of Events and Information	Remarks and references to Appendices
NIEUPORT	29	—	Dull morning cleared in afternoon, usual artillery activity on both sides. Arranged to meet D.M.G.O. re selection of barrage positions. D.M.G.O. was detained, but called at Coy H.Q. in the evening + arranged scheme for evening's guns. Special Coy R.E.'s bombardment again postponed on account of unfavourable conditions. Considerable artillery activity during night on ISLAND POSITIONS necessitating much attention by evening casualties nil. 31 Battery went sick today.	Atty Capt
	30	—	Raised early morning but cleared up later. O.C. inspected positions for Barrage fire + decided to construct new ones. 6 to 8.10 hrs artillery put up S.O.S. lines. Enemy retaliated was replied to by fives of other S.O.S. lines. Enemy retaliation was not very heavy. Night much quieter than usual. Working parties of 30 men from various sections carried on + constructed 16 of new emplacements for barrage scheme. Under 2nd trains. One gun had 4,000 rounds during night.	Major ... att

Mt Gordon Capt.
OC 194 M.G. Coy
31/7/17

199 M.G. Coy.

War Diary

August 1917.

Army Form C. 2118.

WAR DIARY
or
INTELLIGENCE SUMMARY.
(Erase heading not required.)

Page 53

199 Machine Gun Company

August 1917

Place	Date	Hour	Summary of Events and Information	Remarks and references to Appendices
	July 31	—	Dull day. Artillery active both sides. Received orders during afternoon that two sections were to relieve two sections of 219 M.G.Coy in coast defence. Nos 1 and 4 Sections under 2nd Lt Thoma & 2nd Lt Barker from Jean Bart Camp Coxyde were detailed. The two sections in line and H.Q. at Nieuport were relieved about 12 pm. returning to Jean Bart Camp bed. Heavy rain. Our guns very active and during relief fun H.Q. hit very bad.	MJT
	Aug 1		Remainder of Coy relieves remainder of 219 Coy in coast defence. No 3 Section under Lt Parker at Newport Bains, Radf No2 Section under 2nd Lt Barker L.ST Mobile, remaining half section No 2 and H.Q. to Coxyde Bains Relif, complete 2.30 p.m. Weather very bad indeed. Belleck Foot with 50.0 standings for animals. 2nd Lieut Dumfrey and 15 O.R. reinforcements arrived about 5 pm.	MJT
	Aug 2		Very windy and rainy day. Day spent in cleaning up and checking stores etc. during day. C.O. went round gun positions. 2.O.R reinforcements arrived about 5 pm. In the evening received notification to relieve 148 M.G. Coy in Lombartzyde sector, eight guns to move on morning of the fourth and eight on the evening of the fourth. BMG O'Connor to discuss.	MJT
	Aug 3		Again day very windy and wet. Lts Parker, Barker, Daincie & Barber team to reconnoitre tomorrow. C.O. arranged with O.C. 262 M.G.Coy for two of his sections to relieve two of ours by a Coast Defence to enable two sections to relieve two of 148 M.G.Coy in the line.	MJT

Army Form C. 2118.

Page 54

WAR DIARY
or
INTELLIGENCE SUMMARY.

199 Machine Gun Coy

(Erase heading not required.)

Place	Date	Hour	Summary of Events and Information	Remarks and references to Appendices
	Aug 4		303 R & L sections relieved by 202 M.G. Coy and left about 2 a.m. and returned two sections of 148 M.G. Coy, who then proceeded to relieve No 1 & 2 (see O.O. App A.) Relief delayed owing to enemy shelling	App A ReAttached
	Aug 5		Relief not complete until about 8.30 a.m. owing to teams getting separated in the darkness and very heavy shelling. We were very lucky to get in without a single casualty. Casualty Roy for week ending evening August 5. See routine orders attached.	
			Light firing during the day. Shortly after dusk very heavy shelling started from the direction of the Sun position. Shells came over the ridge, some 800 and 25 funnels and roads were all well received a direct hit. 25 funnel and roads were also hit and 2 others injured. 2 horses were shot and 1 attempt to escape at night or runaway.	
				App B
	Aug 6		Rode around brigade reconnoitred caught, corporals with 15 it and return in distance 300 — 5 horses 21 machine guns being taken. (See App B.)	
	Aug 7		Artillery fire active on both sides during the night, a gas projector attack was carried out on enemy trenches in the vicinity of Company Headquarters. A firing or party	

A5834 Wt. W4473 M687 750,000 8/16 D.D. & L. Ltd. Forms/C.2118/13.

Army Form C. 2118.

WAR DIARY
or
INTELLIGENCE SUMMARY.
(Erase heading not required.)

Page 56

199 Machine Gun Coy

Place	Date	Hour	Summary of Events and Information	Remarks and references to Appendices
	Aug 9		Day and night very quiet. 1C went round the REDAN guns with DMGO 32nd Div. (Major Booth) and reconnoitre new positions for the REDAN guns, in order to obtain a better close defence of the REDAN. 2nd LT BARKER relieves by 2nd LONGRAY. Guns fires indirect day and night 9/10 13750 rounds.	
	Aug 10		Day very quiet. Portion of the Low guns in the REDAN attacked. 2nd Lt Thomas relieves Lt Parker about 5.30 pm. Enemy put a barrage on 1st & 2nd lines R+L sectors, also box barrage 9.25 to 11.0 pm. Afterwards night very quiet.	
	Aug 11		Day fairly quiet. Very heavy shelling around REDAN 11.30 p.m. 1 am gas shells also used. 6.0 rounds fired with DMGO mortars gas. Low positions (passages) to advance my guns to say HG gun position. Any place is wanted to take advance SOS lamps position. No casualties one wounded 12.15" wire stopped (Rifle) not known. Guns up to stand 9.30 un'am Aç-am. Russ Lt A3 all morning fired up to about 30. Cases about 10 p.m. 10 am REDAN heavy shelling barrage all ammy used with HMG bombardment guns Rebass lost SOS lines many no trouble with front from about 10 pm 6 t am. L Crescents No 16 gun shell fire and more from — Rifles. 2 Ych. one wounded — R. Res.)	

A5834 Wt. W4973 M687 750,000 8/16 D. D. & L. Ltd. Forms/C.2118/13.

WAR DIARY
or
INTELLIGENCE SUMMARY

Army Form C. 2118.

Page 6

199 Machine Gun Coy

(Erase heading not required.)

Place	Date	Hour	Summary of Events and Information	Remarks and references to Appendices
	13		Day fairly quiet. Duty O reported at 6.30 to discuss with O.C. decided to withdraw three forward guns making four guns in reserve at Coy HQ. 2nd Lieut Bauers reports for duty.	
	14		Casualties Pte Read injured - shellfire (see App 1.)	MH
			Day quiet. During night heavy hostile bombardment. HQ mess with gas shells. Eight men gassed. 5 wounded by shellfire. 2nd Lieut Bauers & 2nd Lieut Ashford report to Coy HQ. for reconnaissance.	MH
	15		Much gas sent into Beaufort at night. After a long quiet day 15 men were gassed when dug-out which had been considered gas proof was penetrated. Afternoon spent reconnoitering with a view into which two MGs had penetrated. Men are very short of water now.	MH
	16		OC of 96th MG Coy & 19 MG Coy forward to arrange relief. After 12 V.s sent to assist under Kellam & Hudson during the day which appeared to be fairly quiet. About two men to four in contact. Target in trenches until gun projectile operators at night.	MH
	17		Day quiet. Busy getting ready for relief. Officers (section) relieving Coy comes to reconnoitre. Relief commenced about 9pm. & proved off very quickly & quietly.	MH

Time off 11.50

WAR DIARY or INTELLIGENCE SUMMARY

Army Form C. 2118.

Page 57

199 Machine Gun Coy

Place	Date	Hour	Summary of Events and Information	Remarks and references to Appendices
	Aug 18		Company left Cocquelle about 12.30 (marched) to Lauberque, then by Lorry to Frévendale, then (marched) to Volenghem. Billetted in Peasants' barn. Apparently getting billets in any area very fine.	MG
	19		Lovely day. Company busy cleaning guns etc. Photo afternoon. Dinner in evening by Major Barnes EE &pm	MG
	20		This day Company inspected in the morning by O.C. Afternoon 5 kits etc inspection. South Thomas & Bray Dunes to get company card. Lieut Aylmer evacuated to CCS 10th Battalion on the result of gun practice. Et Potéz went over duties & 2nd in command and to Barker. Later & Transport Officer. 20 Reinforcements arrived. 19 men billeted to the Company previously.	MG
	21st		One day Company training in the morning. Limber work in the afternoon C.O. and Lt. Francis rode to BRAY DUNES to attend Court of Inquiry, returning in the afternoon.	MG
	22nd		Ordinary day Company training. Coy visited by Major Dartmouth D.A.A.G. who inquired if billets etc were capable. Officers and figures & men inspection in the afternoon. C.O and Lt Potéz rode to Division to interview Major Gedal and G.R.E. and obtain troops.	MG
	23rd		Company inspected by C.O. Morning. Programme interrupted by violent showers. After dinner O.C. inspected Transport. Very good turnout of animals and harness.	MG

Army Form C. 2118.

WAR DIARY
or
INTELLIGENCE SUMMARY

199 Machine Gun Coy

Page 58

(Erase heading not required.)

Instructions regarding War Diaries and Intelligence Summaries are contained in F. S. Regs., Part II. and the Staff Manual respectively. Title pages will be prepared in manuscript.

Place	Date	Hour	Summary of Events and Information	Remarks and references to Appendices
	24/12		Dull day. Major Foster visited Company during the morning & inspected Transport Lines. I.O.R. Reinspected arrived from base. Weather raining & windy and slightly milder afternoon.	AH
	25		Bright Day. Company training during morning. Football during afternoon - S. Hartley rejoined from base.	AH
	26		Wet windy day. Church Service in morning. Afternoon off.	AH
	27		Wet day training in billets. Barrage drill explained. Afternoon fire direction orders.	AH
	28		Wet day training in billets. Barrage drill & Physical training in five intervals.	AH
	29		Wet day training in barrage work practiced. Drill was carried out showing fire intervals.	AH
	30		The first dry morning for some days. Good use was made of the opportunity to go a morning's Barrage work was carried out by all sections. S. Thorpe returned from leave about midday. Took over command of duties of Transport Officer. Major Foster D.D.V.S. inspected our animals during afternoon. Strength of Company 12 officers & 141 O.R.	AH

[signature] Captn.
O.C. 199 M.G. Coy

199th MACHINE GUN Co.
No.
Date

Appx. B

199 Machine Gun Coy

M.G.5.
2/8/17

Report of Machine Gun Operations carried out by this Coy in Co-operation with a raid by the 6th W.R.R. on enemy trenches on night 7/8th Aug 17

1. <u>This Coy was detailed</u> to co-operate with four guns, providing barrage fire on Area M 23 a 3.9 – M 17 c 30.60 – M 17 c 90.00 · M 17 c 80.55 and to enfilade LORRY LANE from M 17 c 9.0 to M 17 c 80.55. see 147 Inf. Bde. O.O. No 102

2. <u>Disposition</u>. For this purpose I decided to use my Right Sections' Guns bringing the 'Corner House' & 'Canal Bank' guns back to positions close by existing "Roadside" guns. i.e. I had all my guns at the side of the road 20 yards apart at M 29 c 65.25

3. <u>Control</u>. I detailed one officer to each sub-section of two guns.

4. <u>Direction and Elevation</u>:- this was maintained by use of new night firing screens which proved very satisfactory.

5. <u>Ammo. Supply</u>.- Belts were filled as emptied by spare Nos. in Section Dug out

6. <u>Fire</u>:- Opened at 1 a.m. (ZERO) Rate 150 Rds until ZERO+10, from +10 to +50 Rate 50 Rds. Fire was ceased temporarily at 1.50 A.M. then one gun was detailed to carry on firing on LOMBARTZYDE until dawn & the other 3 swung back on to their S.O.S. lines.

7. <u>General</u>: Guns worked extremely well – no mechanical stoppages whatever – 5 mins after ZERO enemy shells burst along Canal Bank direct to our front & later a hostile M.G. fired a few rounds in direction of our gun positions N.C.O's & men behaved excellently & showed common-sense throughout firing

N.F. Gadsden Capt
O.C. 199 M.G. Coy

War Diary. Vol 10

of

1991 Machine Gun Cory

September 1917

WAR DIARY / INTELLIGENCE SUMMARY

Page 59

Army Form C. 2118.

199 Machine Gun Company

Place	Date	Hour	Summary of Events and Information	Remarks and references to Appendices
	26/8/17		A fine morning. Barrage drill. Capt Gadsdon to Divison during morning. Afternoon football. Night operations 9 P.M – 11.30 P.M.	RA/M¹
	1/9/17		A good days training. A fine morning. Coy paraded & inspection at 9 am. A few turn out still room for improvement.	RA/M¹ CW/P¹
	2/9/17		Divine Service by Major Barnes C.F. A very windy day.	CW/A¹
	3/9/17		A fine days training. Reserved Barrage drill again carried out.	CW/P¹
	4/9/17		Another fine days Barrage drill. Training as usual.	CW/P¹ CW/A¹
	5/9/17		Another very wet day. Coy moved to SES & Company Battled Does during afternoon	CW/P¹ CW/A¹
	6/9/17		A heavy gas bomb shell during morning. Quite successful	CW/P¹
			A heavy gas barrage solvent T.O.E.T. &c during morning. Two officers attended lecture on gas barrage solvent of barrage at gas school. 148 M.G. Coy during afternoon. Capt. Gadsdon to D.is artillery proceeding to reconnoitre for two days. He is attached to D.is artillery	CW/P¹ CW/A¹
	7/9/17		T.O.E.T & gun drill during morning. Capt. Gadsdon to D.is artillery to study their Barrage methods. Received orders to move to Bray Dunes.	CW/P¹ CW/A¹
	8/9/17		Coy moved to Bray Dunes. Move complete 8.30 P.M. Good billets & horse lines. Coy congratulated by Divl. General on its appearance turn out	CW/P¹
	9/9/17		Day spent in cleaning up & refreshing for divisional horse show & inspection by O.C. Divs Green No 1. See Co operated with 147 Brigade in Brigade manoeuvres	CW/P¹

WAR DIARY or INTELLIGENCE SUMMARY

Army Form C. 2118.

Page 6

Place	Date	Hour	Summary of Events and Information	Remarks and references to Appendices
Happy Valley Buire	14/9/17		The Coy secured a first in the divisional horse show for team out of units timber. This is satisfactory as very little time was allowed for preparation.	(3)P/-
	12/9/17		Coy training on new training area.	(4)P/-
			NCH section attached to 14th I.B. for manoeuvres with infantry. Remainder of Coy practising close support of infantry. Transport inspected by O.C. Div. Train. Quite a few horse cast.	(4)P/-
	14/9/17		Coy took part in brigade operations under orders of 148 brigade. Coy did a creeping barrage to 14th & 15th & Coy previously the close support.	
	15/9/17		Review this morning. Co. Coy fired 25 bkoyds. Afternoon to see inspection of Held. & Football during the evening.	(5)R/-
	16/9/17		Sunday Church service was held during morning. News received that the Company had won first prize at the Corps show for our two set of mules & another prizes reduced to move to Hordel to be close them Bray Dunes by 10 am 17th.	(6)P/-
	17/9/17 "		Company moved to first camp at Gyvell them Bray Dunes. Horses in two open lines complete by noon.	(6)P/-
	18/9/17		Continued canal and general training. A wet day.	(7)P/-
	19/9/17		Lorry work. No 2 section took part in brigade exercise under 146 brigade.	(8)P/-
	20/9/17		Barrack work.	(9)P/4
	21/9/17		Coy fired barrage into the sea. Good observation was obtained & good results very satisfactory.	Copy

Page 61

WAR DIARY
or
INTELLIGENCE SUMMARY.
(Erase heading not required.)

Army Form C. 2118.

Place	Date	Hour	Summary of Events and Information	Remarks and references to Appendices
	22/9/17		Barrage work	B/Pr C/Pr
	23/9/17		Barrage work. Coy received orders to move to LEDERZEELE area on 24th.	R/Pr C/Pr
	24/9/17		Coy proceeded to billets in LEDERZEELE area. Move complete by 2 P.M. Coy moved in lorries. Transport moved by road on 23rd inst. Capt. Galston proceeded to CAMIERS to witness barrage demonstration. Afternoon cleaning & oiling limbers.	C/Pr
	25/9/17		Barrage work.	C/Pr
	26/9/17		Barrage work. All Company but a hot bath at billets near BRAEMAR. Capt Galston returned from CAMIERS.	U/Pr
	27/9/17		Received orders to move on 28th inst. to billets in WESTBECOURT area. Limbers packed.	C/Pr
	28/9/17		Coy moved to billets at WESTBECOURT. A long march (18 miles). The Company arrived very well. Move complete 6 P.M. Good billets.	C/Pr
	29/9/17		Capt. Galston proceeded to CAMIERS to attend 48 A Vickers course at 2 P.M. Spent School Day. After cleaning off & oiling of greasing limbers.	C/Pr Pr C/Pr
	30/9/17		Coy took part in Divisional Tactical Scheme, moving off from billets at 6.0 a.m. & returning in the afternoon. Very hot day. Lt-Col. leaving DH90. inspected Transport Lines.	C/Pr

From O.C. 199 M.G. Coy
To Headquarters
41st Division (G)

Herewith Diary for the month
of October 1917

                    W.H. Gadsden
                        Capt
                Comdg 199 M.G. Coy

WAR DIARY or INTELLIGENCE SUMMARY

Army Form C. 2118.

199.M.G.Coy.

Ref: BELGIUM 1/100,000 HAZEBROUCK
BELGIUM 1/40,000 Sheet 28.

Place	Date	Hour	Summary of Events and Information	Remarks and references to Appendices
	October 1917			
	1.		Company moved from billets at WESTBECOURT at 3 p.m. to CORMETTE. Motor Transport moved ahead, but halted owing to accident with Rapid Cart. Arrived at CORMETTE early in the evening. H.Q. in Chateau.	W.A.
	2.		Company moved at 8.30 a.m. to BAVINCHOVE, near CASSEL. Fell out for 1½ hours halt - for lunch at CLAIRMARAIS forest. Arrived in billets about 4.30 p.m. Company and settled down for night.	W.A.
	3.		Moved to TRAPPISTES, near WATOU. Coy. billeted in farm of Trappists' Monastery where 14th Bde. Headquarters were situated. Very tiring march, as units were constantly halting in front.	W.A.
	4.		Morning spent in cleaning up and rifle inspection. In the afternoon, the Company reported ammunition belts for the line; officers did compass work under O.C.	W.A.
	5.		Morning spent preparing guns and packing limbers. The Company paraded on the POPERINGHE road at 2.45 p.m. for an emergency tour.	

WAR DIARY
or
INTELLIGENCE SUMMARY.

(Erase heading not required.)

Army Form C. 2118.

199. M.G. Coy.

Place	Date	Hour	Summary of Events and Information	Remarks and references to Appendices
	5th	7.30 p.m.	The lorries failed to appear until 7.30.p.m. Coy moved into the line to relieve the (Divisional) NEW ZEALAND M.G. Company who were occupying S.O.S. positions in the PASSCHENDAELE sector. Guide was picked up at the Asylum, YPRES and Coy. proceeded up ST JEAN — WIELTJE Road. Traffic was closeded and the state of the roads very bad. After much difficulty the relief was completed on the morning of the 6th about 6.a.m. 40 men of the West Yorks Regiment were attached for carrying purposes.	Ref:- Report on visit of 199 Coy. M.G.C. to Salient (attached) M.V.
	6th		Day spent in reconnoitring forward positions and settling down. It proved to be fraught with great difficulty owing to S.O.S. & to forward dumps, experiencing great difficulty with pack animals on account of mud and water.	M.V.
	7		Very cold and raining. All stand to the S.O.S. was sent up on the evening and Divisional Front. Batteries promptly opened fire. 110,000 was sent up on the Divisional Front. Batteries promptly opened fire. 170,000 Rounds.	M.V.

WAR DIARY
or
INTELLIGENCE SUMMARY.

(Erase heading not required.)

Army Form C. 2118.

199 M.G. Coy

Place	Date	Hour	Summary of Events and Information	Remarks and references to Appendices
	OCTOBER 1917			
	8th		Morning spent in working out barrage charts etc., and carrying till completed. Guns were brought up and new lines of fire laid out, about 3.0.p.m. The enemy shelled the slopes of GRAVENSTAFEL RIDGE and created casualties in the gun teams. Shelling was continued till 10.30.p.m. The teams were reorganised during the night, and prepared to mount and lay guns at daybreak.	M.A.
	9th		Division attacked at 5.20.a.m. All guns were in position to open fire at ZERO, except 3, one of which had been blown up. (Replaced: the two remaining had lost their gun commanders and most of their personnel. Over 100,000 rounds were fired; after the barrage had ceased, S.O.S. lines were taken up. During the afternoon the D.M.G.O. sent information to the C.O. that enemy was massing for a counter attack on	M.A.

WAR DIARY
or
INTELLIGENCE SUMMARY

Army Form C. 2118.

199. M.G. Coy.

OCTOBER 1917

Place	Date	Hour	Summary of Events and Information	Remarks and references to Appendices
FRIESLAND COPSE.	9		Barrage was despatched to battery positions and in 15 minutes fire was brought to bear on the above target. This brought hostile retaliation, as a result of which no one casualties occurred, and 3 guns were put out of action. The S.O.S. went up about plenty to be in the evening and all guns again fired.	C.H.P.
	10		Fire was maintained intermittently throughout the night. Day spent in getting up S.a.a. Total amount of ammunition carried to gun positions = 300,000 rounds, S.a.a 200,000 rounds fired from ZERO hour until time of heading over. About 4.30 p.m. enemy opened up on battery positions. Again shelled for. Hostile shelling put 2 guns of No 3 section	

WAR DIARY
or
INTELLIGENCE SUMMARY.
(Erase heading not required.)

Army Form C. 2118.

199 M.G. Coy.

OCT. 1917

Place	Date	Hour	Summary of Events and Information	Remarks and references to Appendices
	10th		out of action, and reduced their personnel to 5 men. This section was therefore, withdrawn the Coy were relieved by the 2nd N.Z. M.G. Coy during the night.	[initials]
	11th		Company assembled in X Camp, ST JEAN, where not to had been bivouacked. After a short halt, Coy marched to transport lines, W. of YPRES, had dinners, and proceeded to WARRINGTON CAMP, near BRAND HOEK: very comfortable billets.	[initials]
	12th		Day spent in cleaning up, sorting gunpit and equipment and treating bad feet. Were advised with news that Lance-Corporal A.J. WHITE, No 2 section, had been awarded the Military Medal	[initials]
	13th		Coy engaged in getting straight and adjusting deficiencies of Kit and Clothing.	[initials]

Army Form C. 2118.

WAR DIARY
or
INTELLIGENCE SUMMARY.
(Erase heading not required.)

199. M.G. Coy

OCT. 1917.

Place	Date	Hour	Summary of Events and Information	Remarks and references to Appendices
	14th		Sunday. Service in Transport Billet conducted by Major Barnes. Afternoon resting.	CWS
	15		Work on limbers in the morning. Pay in the afternoon, and limber packing for move.	A.B.
	16th		Coy. moved to Billets near WINNEZEELE at 8.30 a.m. though POPERINGHE and ABEELE. A great deal of Artillery was moving in the same direction: this caused many blocks and delays. A halt for lunch was observed 1½ kilometres East of STEENVOORDE. Arrived in Billets 5 p.m.	CWS
	17th		Day spent in cleaning limbers and settling down in new Billets. Visit by D.H.G.O. in the morning.	CWS

A5834. Wt. W4973 M687. 750,000. 8/16 D.D. & L. Ltd. Forms/C.2118/13.

WAR DIARY
or
INTELLIGENCE SUMMARY
(Erase heading not required.)

Army Form C. 2118.

199 M.G. Coy.

Oct 1917

Place	Date	Hour	Summary of Events and Information	Remarks and references to Appendices
	18th		Training Commenced. Gun work in the morning and bombing in the afternoon. Attached men formed into Squads under capable N.C.O's for elementary instruction.	Apx 1
	19th		Coy training the whole day. Special classes for Junior N.C.O's under 2nd Lt BARKER started.	Apx 2
	20th		Coy inspected by C.O. in the morning. Visit by D.A.Q.G., who changed word - drawing R.Q.	Apx 3
	21st		Church parade at 11 a.m conducted by Rev. F.R. BARNES. Remainder of the day very quiet.	Apx 4
	22nd		Day spent in training and preparing numbers for transport inspection.	Apx 5
	23rd		Coy at baths in the afternoon. Divisional Band played on the Football Ground from 3-4/15.	Apx 6

WAR DIARY
or
INTELLIGENCE SUMMARY.

(Erase heading not required.)

Army Form C. 2118.

199 M.G. Coy D.T./4

Vol XI

Place	Date	Hour	Summary of Events and Information	Remarks and references to Appendices
	23/4		Training as per programme	
	24/4		— " —	
	25/4		— " —	
	26/4		— " — Limbers issued for move	
	27/4		Coy moved to TAUSGAT STEENVOORD. Good billets. Coy settled in by 3 PM. at 6 PM orders received that Coy was transferred to 18th Div. & was to move by 6 A.M. 28th	
	28/4	6 AM	Coy moved to WORMHOUDT. Very excellent billets. Left "Gardson bejours" of the Company	
			Coy moved to BRAY DUNES. An excellent march & again very lucky will billets	
			in a few days. Weaving off & getting straight after the move. G.O.C.	
			...thanked the Company for working so rippingly	

R Wrawby Lt. Adjt.
199 M.G. Coy

R Wrawby Lt. adjt
199 M.G. Coy

Report of operations carried out by the 199th Machine Gun Company during period 5th - 11th October, 1917.

The Company relieved the New Zealand Divisional Machine Gun Company on the 5th/6th experiencing great difficulty in getting into position owing to the crowded state of roads up to SPREE Farm, and the terrible condition of the track after that place. The relieving guides were at a most unsuitable place necessitating a detour of some 200 yards, really a hours journey with our loads
Relief finally completed about 6-0 am on the 6th instant.

The relieved Company only provided two guides for the Coy. which was of course absurd, and caused several hours delay especially as the night was very dark.
The 6th was spent settling in, getting up ammunition and reconnoitring forward battery positions.
At stand to on the evening of the 7th the S.O.S went up along the whole divisional front, all guns opening with gratifying promptness, and about 40,000 rounds were fired. As the S.O.S. was not repeated fire gradually slowed down and ceased.
'A' battery completed their gun emplacement on the forward battery positions during the night of the 6th/7th. 'B' battery who were not quite so exposed to view working during the forenoon of the 7th and finished their positions before noon. The afternoon was spent in getting up A.S.S. AA
The 8th was spent working out calculations for barrage and getting forward S.A.A. This was extremely hard work and it was found impossible to get the A.S.S. forward in boxes, we were finally reduced to unpacking the ammunition and sending it up in bandoliers repacking into boxes on the battery position in order to keep it clean.
We commenced bringing up the guns about 3-0 pm. in the afternoon and laying out lines of fire.
The enemy opened rather heavily on the slope of GRAVESTRAVEL RIDGE and dispersed several of our gun teams, causing casualties. Shelling was kept up till about 10-30 pm. All officers of the Company spent the night reorganising the teams and preparing to mount and lay guns at the first glimpse of light. Rain was falling heavily, which hampered our efforts and there was very little moon.
Guns were laied at the break of dawn and all was ready to open at the Zero hour with the exception of three guns, one of which was punctured by shrapnel and the other two guns teams had lost their gun Commander and most of the personnel.
After I had ascertained that all available guns could be mounted and laid by Zero hour I left battery position and reported to 148 Brigade Headquarters.
The thirteen available guns opened fire at Zero.
At this point I should like to mention that a note was received at 11-30 pm. on the night of the 8th/9th altering all the barrage scheme. As it was quite impossible to get my Battery Commanders together and alter all our arrangements, I sent a note to each Commander to carry on with the old scheme making a few necessary alterations in the times.
Battery Commanders had been advises to use their discretion as to ceasing fire with certain guns and overhauling them, this was done commencing about Z plus 30. Not more than one gun per battery being out of action at a time.
The rate of fire worked out as low as 40/50 rounds per minute. This of course was owing to the conditions.. Many No.3.stoppages occured through wet belts and grit. It was found necessary in most cases to increase weight of fuzee springs about 2 lbs.
I calculated and found by checking ammunition before and after the barrage that over 100,000 rounds were fired.

- 2 -

Control was established by Batteries, each battery having three officers, i.e. a battery Commander and one officer per Section. Section Officers were all supplied with duplicate Battery Commanders Charts but watched Battery Commander for signals and repeated to their Section. I was in touch with Batteries by means of runners, who were really excellent. The whole system of control worked well from start to finish.

After the barrage had been fired and the S.O.S. lines taken up I withdrew two officers per battery and established 8 hour watches. This unfortunately could not be done in the case of the men as ammunition was still urgently required.

During afternoon of t e 9th. I received information from D.M.G.O. that the enemy were massing for a counter attack behind FREESLAND ? Copse. I had carefully prepared for such an eventuallity and all officers had been practiced in getting guns to bear on target at short notice. I despatched a runner immediately ordering all guns so any degrees right of chart concentration and giving the Q.E. This worked excellently, about 900 yards of difficult country was covered by the runner and fire brought to bear in 15 minutes. This unfortunately evoked considerable relatiation from the enemy and a very bad hours bombardment ensued, during which we lost heavily in men and also had three guns put out of action.
The S.O.S. when up about stand to that night and again all available guns opened. This was particularly gratifying as most of the guns had been nearly buried by mud and dirt thrown up by shells and speaks well for the work of the Nos 1. in getting their guns cleaned up.
About 4-0 pm. a message was received from the D.M.G.O. to fire intermittently all night and reduce S.O.S. line 300^x this was done.
About 8-0 pm. the D.M.G.O. rang me up and asked me to extend range of S.O.S. again to original limit. This was done and fire maintained a night. The whole of the 10th was spent in getting up ammunition ready to hand over. 100,000 rounds was got up making a total carried up to the gun positions of 300,000 of which 200,000 was fired from zero to the hour of handing over. About 4-30 pm. the enemy opened up on our battery positions with heavy shell, our guns opened fire as they were of opinion that a S.O.S. had gone up. The enemy's fire put two guns of No.3. Section out of action and reduced their available personnel to five men. I therefore withdrew the section leaving 3 sections in the battery positions.
Visual signalling might have been employed had a field box been available for the forward signallers. The only one there was, was the taken by the Brigade, who required the whole of it for their signals and O.P. As it was the system of runners worked well.
Too little information was available as to the disposition and forming up points of our own Infantry. At zero hour troops passed through our batteries in artillery formation causing some delay in our fire.
The attached men were sent to us much too late to be of much assistance and we received them just as we were consequently cunfusion was caused trying to allot them to sections in the streets of YPRES.
Not sufficient guide boards were available to point the way to dressing stations and I am of opinion that this lack probably caused the death fo many men, who otherwise might have found their way back.

www.ingramcontent.com/pod-product-compliance
Lightning Source LLC
Chambersburg PA
CBHW081551160426
43191CB00011B/1895